General Salute

Attention Authors

'We Convert Fighters into Writers.' That's the motto of Manas Publications since more than four decades. Our message to the world is that India can win the battle not only by the bullet but also by the pen. There is no dearth of intellectuals in our country, but their knowledge is confined to them only. No sincere effort has been made by any other publisher to channelise their knowledge in national interest. That is why the talent of a large number of intellectuals remains latent. An author transforms his knowledge into a manuscript, and it is our job to spread his/her knowledge by converting it into a beautiful book. For over four decades, Manas has been motivating the intellectuals by publishing their manuscripts and would like to publish your manuscript too. So if you or your colleagues have any manuscript ready for publication or are working on it, kindly contact us with detailed synopsis and list of contents. We will transform your work into a valuable publication. If you wish, we can also suggest you the suitable subjects for writing the books related to your area of expertise. Manas is known for its publishing quality and commitments. We take utmost care in production and give wide publicity to the book as well as its author through our national and international distribution network.

General Salute

Lt Col Arun Jha
(Retd)

Manas Publications
(We Convert Fighters into Writers)
New Delhi-110002 (INDIA)

MANAS PUBLICATIONS
(We Convert Fighters into Writers)
(Publishers, Library Suppliers, Importers and Exporters)
4402/5-A, Ansari Road (Opp. HDFC Bank)
Darya Ganj, New Delhi-110 002 (India)
Off. (23260783, 23265523, Fax: 011-23272766
E-mail: manaspublications@vsnl.com
manaspublications@gmail.com

ISBN 978-81-7049-437-9
₹ 495/-

Designed at
Manas Publications

Printed in India at
HS Offset Press, Delhi
and published by Mrs Suman Lata for
Manas Publications, 4402/5-A, Ansari Road
(Opp. HDFC Bank),
Darya Ganj, New Delhi-110 002 (INDIA)

Contents

Preface

Army as a profession is par excellence. I feel that every individual must undergo Army training to enhance his/her personality. One's exposure to the multifaceted adventurous Army life is a great learning for life. It fills one with courage to take any challenge in life smilingly and come out triumphant. The fast-paced, exciting military life also serves as a good lesson for the Army officer's family for adapting quickly to any circumstances.

I donned the Army colours for a long time and sincerely discharged whatever duties were given to me. However, being a former Army officer, I felt a great pain seeing some General officers damaging the Army's good reputation by their highly selfish, corrupt acts. Never in the past so many General officers showed moral bankruptcy as today.

The thought of writing a book never occurred to me until General VK Singh filed his statutory complaint in the last week of August, 2011. I kept dilly-dallying penning down my straightforward thoughts and views about my life in the Army till the 16th of January 2012, when General VK Singh approached the Supreme Court to justify his claim, not supported by facts, on his date of birth. The highly self-motivated conduct of the General on the verge of his retirement strengthened my resolve to write the book, and the result is in your hands. The sole aim of writing this book is to tell the common man how could an individual subject the great institution of Army to the ridicule by the media and people for his own gains.

The Army Chief Gen VK Singh too threw the Army ethos and values to the wind by moving the Supreme Court, banking on his date of birth (DOB) claim. By going back on his earlier commitments regarding his DOB, the Army Chief subjected the great institution of Army to the ridicule by the media and people. The Supreme Court did not see any merit in the General's claim on age and advised him to withdraw his petition. Though finally the General heeded to the Supreme Court's advice, his behaviour was no better than those politicians who somehow want to cling to their chairs for life. The General's selfish behaviour is detrimental for the internal health of the Indian Army. Interestingly, he later on stated that the apex court has created more confusion without addressing the main issue. Undoubtedly, this is an irresponsible insinuations with reference to court proceedings.

As I do not want to sensationalize certain critical issues, I drew a *Lakshman Rekha* to ensure that my views must not dent the image of this great institution. Purposely, I refrained from broaching certain ills plaguing the Indian

Army. By delving into these ills I do not want to put my brother officers at a disadvantage, though I hope that senior officers will take cue from this book to cure these ills. I refrained from touching upon any issue for which I did not have any documentary evidence. Also, I did not bring out any issue which is based on 'hearsay'.

I have brought out many gross acts of impropriety committed by some General officers with utter disregard of the Army rule book without caring for the depth of the whirlpool I am plunging into this by writing this book. I am going ahead with it as my conscience demands it. The Indian Army no longer remains a profession of popular choice though since time immemorial it was a profession which people joined purely out of passion. General VK Singh in his bid to gain 10 months' extension lost sight of the fact what impact his age row would have on the youth's prospects of joining the Indian Army. Sad! Because of certain shocking revelations, the book will make an interesting reading for both the uniformed personnel and common readers. The objective of this disclosure is to initiate a rethink in the Army for putting in place an effective system for isolating and punishing the corrupt among its ranks.

Lt Col Arun Jha (retd)
(arunjha67@rediffmail.com)
+919582044400

Note: The letters, other documents and the Allahabad High Court judgement reproduced in this book have some footnotes which were not part of their original versions. The author has added these footnotes to express his views on certain important developments to highlight certain key issues.

Acknowledgements

My family who stood by me throughout my Army career and my eldest daughter, Miss Anubhuti Jha for having edited and vetted this book.

Dedicated to

Soldiers of Indian Army for their dedication to Motherland.

List of Abbreviations

2IC	-	Second-in-Command
AA	-	Army Act
ACR	-	Annual Confidential Report
Add	-	Addition
Addl	-	Additional
Adjt	-	Adjutant
Admn	-	Administrative
AFT	-	Armed Forces Tribunal
AG	-	Adjutant General
AMS	-	Assistant Military Secretary
AN	-	Afternoon
AO	-	Army Order
ARTRAC	-	Army Training Command

Arty	-	Artillery
ATG	-	Annual Training Grant
AWWA	-	Army Wives Welfare Association
Bde	-	Brigade
BM	-	Brigade Major
Bn	-	Battalion
Br	-	Branch
Brig	-	Brigadier
BRO	-	Battalion Routine Order
C/L	-	Casual Leave
Cdr	-	Commander
Clk	-	Clerk
CO	-	Commanding Officer
COAS	-	Chief of the Army Staff
COI	-	Court of Inquiry
Col	-	Colonel
Comdt	-	Commandant
Coy	-	Company
CR	-	Confidential Report
CSD	-	Central Stores Depot
CT	-	Counter Terrorism
Dep	-	Departure
DGMO	-	Director General of Military Operations
Dist	-	District
Distr	-	Distribution
Div	-	Division
DO	-	Demi Official
DOB	-	Date of Birth
Docu	-	Document

DSSC	-	Defence Services Staff College
ERE	-	Extra Regimental Employability
Est	-	Establishment
Fwd	-	Forward
Gen	-	General
GSO	-	General Staff Officer
HC	-	Higher Command
HC	-	High Court
HM	-	Hizbul Mujaheedin
HQ	-	Headquarters
IED	-	Improvised Explosive Device
IG	-	Inspector General
IMA	-	Indian Military Academy
IMF	-	Indian Mountaineering Federation
Incl	-	Include
Inf	-	Infantry
Instr	-	Instructor
Int	-	Intelligence
IPKF	-	Indian Peace Keeping Force
ITC	-	Individual Training Cycle
JC	-	Junior Command
LC	-	Line of Control
Ldr	-	Leader
LO	-	Liaison Officer
Lt Col	-	Lieutenant Colonel
Maj	-	Major
MCN	-	Military Credit Note
MMG	-	Medium Machine Gun
MOD	-	Ministry of Defence
Mov	-	Movement

MS	-	Military Secretary
MTO	-	Mechanical Transport Officer
NCO	-	Non - Commissioned Officer
NDA	-	National Defence Academy
NDL	-	National Defence College
Nk	-	Naik
No	-	Number
NOO	-	Not on Original
Obj	-	Objective
Offg	-	Officiating
Offr	-	Officer
OLQ	-	Officer Like Qualities
OP	-	Operation
Org	-	Organisation
OS	-	Office Superintendent
PD	-	Principal Director
PMR	-	Pre Mature Retirement
PM	-	Prime Minister
Prep	-	Prepare
Pt	-	Point
RandR	-	Research and Referral
Rd	-	Road
Ref	-	Refer
Regmt	-	Requirement
Reqd	-	Required
Restd.	-	Restricted
Rif	-	Rifle
RM	-	Raksha Mantri
RO	-	Reviewing Officer
RR	-	Rashtriya Rifles

Rtd	-	Retired
RTI	-	Right to Information
RTU	-	Returned to Unit
S.O.S.	-	Struck off Strength
SC	-	Supreme Court
Sect	-	Sector
Sep	-	Sepoy
Ser	-	Serial
SF	-	Separated Family
SFF	-	Special Frontier Force
SI	-	Senior Instructor
Sig	-	Signal
Sit	-	Situation
SM	-	Sena Medal
SO	-	Staff Officer
Sp	-	Support
SPL	-	Special
SRO	-	Senior Reporting Officer
Stat	-	Statutory
Str	-	Strength
Tele	-	Telephone
Tps	-	Troops
Trg	-	Training
Trn	-	Terrain
VCOS	-	Vice Chief of Army Staff
VSM	-	Vishisht Seva Medal
W/o	-	Without Relief
WHAMP	-	Winning Hearts and Minds of People
YSM	-	Yudh Seva Medal

CHAPTER 1

Army: A Way of Life

Childhood Dream

The sight of an Indian Army officer is always one that impresses – the well-ironed olive green uniform, medals on the chest, epaulettes on the shoulders that speak of an officer's rank and bravery, the upright bearing and the forceful stride. All these signs are enough to make one dream of joining the Army.

Boys by their very nature want to be soldiers or cops. They don't play Mickey and Minnie Mouse in their backyards. Rather, they play GI Joe, Cops and Robbers – tough and rugged games in which good guys are pitted against bad guys. Hence, basically every boy in his childhood gets fascinated by the sight of uniformed soldiers. To some extent, even parents encourage their sons to become soldiers with the aim of instilling in them the values that are intrinsic to a soldier – courage, honour, bravery, integrity, teamwork and love for country.

Army Career – A Career Cut Above the Rest

The bravest are surely those who have the clearest vision of what is before them, glory and danger alike, and yet notwithstanding, go out to meet it.

— **Thucydides**

Career in the Army is one of pride and honour. You stand out in the crowd with your impressive bearing and impeccable conduct. The Army makes a gentleman out of a man. It's not a mundane nine-to-five job. It is a career about safety, honour and pride of India. One joins the Army to boost one's pride, self-respect, self-esteem, dignity and honour. By taking on the risks and hazards inherent in a soldier's life, one wants to prove to others, especially the peers, that one possesses better leadership traits. That is why soldier is cut above the rest.

There is never a dull moment in Army life since the Academy days of a soldier. During training every day is a new day, full of activities. It is while undergoing training that one understands that there is no limit to human endurance. You brave it out the whole day and make it to your bed safe and sound. The training years at National Defence Academy are worth in gold. Training period is rigorous, yet interesting and meaningful. It equips the soldier with the invaluable abilities and values that enable him/her to select any 'trajectory and target' in life and achieve it against all odds.

Much of military training is about experiential learning and grooming. Socialisation is a way of life which is markedly different from any other sphere of life. Life-long you recall training years with utmost satisfaction and contentment.

Naam and *Nishan* is held in reverence by all the soldiers. *Paltan ki Izaat* is the only concern for a soldier while on or away from duty. No army in the world can boast of such splendid and brave troops as the Indian Army. Among many professional armies of the world, the Indian Army has won the laurels and made the country proud by serving tirelessly in the United Nations peace keeping missions. At home also, the Indian soldiers, down the ages, have earned the respect of the society as defenders of the nation and its people. All surveys have rated soldiering as the top profession acceptable to the people, and the Army remains the least corrupt institution.

Army Innings - Challenging and Demanding

The Army career is demanding and challenging, as it comes with many responsibilities towards the nation. Army is not just about being physically fit but it is also about being mentally robust to implement any challenging tasks. Right from the academy training days, the challenges are there in abundance to undertake. Competitiveness is ingrained in one's soul to bring out the best from within. Performance on the war front is another big challenge. Facing the enemy and winning a war is a challenge which is provided to a selected few.

The commitment towards the country is a challenge as it demands your life and limb by going beyond the call of the duty. It reflects in the popular saying - 'For your tomorrow, the soldier sacrifices his today'. For a true soldier, motherland becomes the first priority. A soldier sacrifices a lot on personal and family fronts. All his/her sacrifices are worth in gold as his/her service to the Motherland is in the purest form.

The Indian Army has time and again lived up to its tradition of valour, heroism, sacrifice and fortitude. It stands on vigil along the border, prepared for any sacrifice so that the people of the country may live in peace and with honour. The Indian Army is that and much more. No other profession offers the same opportunities for living a full life as does the military — comradeship, healthy, clean and honourable conditions of work, organised mess life, closeness to nature, travel throughout this marvellous country, facilities for sports, facilities to develop hobbies, and an ethos wherein self-sacrifice is a professional necessity.

Vast Scope of Career

The Army teaches you not only the art of war but also engineering, medicine, law, human resource development and man management. The career scope is immensely wide for both men and women along with growth on both personal and professional fronts. By attending various courses of instruction, one remains abreast with the latest in the field of technology. To satiate the soldier's quest for knowledge, the two-year study leave is a golden opportunity.

Born to Lead

Leadership has no substitute. Douglas McArthur said, "A true leader has the confidence to stand alone, the courage to make tough decisions and the compassion to listen to the needs of his men. He does not set out to become a leader, but become one by the quality of his actions and by integrity of his intent". These words so aptly apply to the soldier in letter and spirit. A soldier is mentally robust and physically tough. He/she epitomizes the age-old adage - when the going gets tough, the tough gets going. Army person is also a thorough gentleman. For a soldier, intelligence is as essential as physical fitness. In other words, *veerta aur vivek* is the crux of the personality traits. While displaying bravery, the soldier is expected to remain calm and cool from within so that the men under his/her command do not suffer any casualty. Rational and analytical thinking coupled with strategies to go about the plan and then stick to it against all odds is essential.

We the Army People

A soldier, a simple villager who has grown up in a humble and modest way, is an epitome of sacrifice. He brings to the Army rich family traditions. And, in return, the Army with its deep and valuable work culture, tradition and system transforms this villager into a man of action with a sense of purpose and a value system. As a result, the simple villager imbibes the commitment to willingly lay down his life for his comrades, his officers, his army and his country. The simple villager's remarkable transformation is proof that the Army can justifiably be proud of its work culture, tradition and system that insulates it from turbulences, pulls and pressures of the civil society.

The soldier remains alert and active throughout his/her career, thanks to the varied roles he/she plays. The very fact that one keeps moving from one place to another every two years makes one remain rejuvenated forever. The lifestyle of a soldier and his family is entirely different from the civvie world. They live in a world of their own where they make merry in their own way.

What makes army life a charmed one is the abundance of good humour and good cheer (and here I mean the 'spiritless' one). Here nobody is too old to let down his/her hair if the Queen of Sheba so demands in a Mess party. A pleasant sight to see COs and 2ICs scrambling in the mad rush all around. Youngsters of unit raiding newly married couples house is a must. And one is delighted not to be spared. Sudden picnics are planned, in group outing to see a movie, shopping expeditions in small groups, rain dances, barbeque parties with bon-fire, husbands' nights etc, etc are all arranged on the spur of the moment to take off the stress of living in a secluded world.

Looking after the guests (socializing has taken a back seat, courtesy modern day gizmos) is very much part of the

Army life. This is mainly due to the fact that one is bound to bump into an acquaintance due to different postings and because the armed forces fraternity is, after all, a small one. Mainly, due to its rich ethos and values- entertaining unexpected guests, that once seemed nerve-racking and impossible, later becomes a pleasure. When a new officer moves in the neighbourhood and is busy unpacking or an old neighbour has sent off their luggage on being posted out, it is ensured that they get all the help. A common phenomenon that each of us face during postings to new station. This way the chain of good Samaritans grows.

Social Status

All of us have our own opinions about what constitutes 'social status'. However it is an undisputed fact that the status of a 'warrior' has stood the test of time. History and society have both held the soldier in high esteem and offered him a unique status in society. By joining the Army, one becomes a member of an exclusive and elite brotherhood, which is the envy of one and all.

Fauji Kid Special

- Born in a Military Hospital.
- Went school in Shaktiman (not TV serial one).
- Jeeps and Jongas were regular mode of transport - no looking up with awe!
- Alternative to Kendriya Vidyalaya (Central School) was Army School.
- The entire family could survive in a one-room temporary quarter with 25 trunks, wooden crates and a dog.
- Smell of brasso and shoe polish is a regular staple.
- Mess was not the one created in the kid's room but the place for soft drink on father's bar chit, which featured in the Mess Bill of the Army officer with details of 'evening out'.

- Children attend many "May Queen" before they knew what Miss India is.
- Their mother often went for Ladies Club and family welfare meets.
- Geru-chuna was all around to make them know that a VIP visit was due.
- Kids knew small towns like Mhow, Wellington, Lansdowne, Deolali and Sagar.
- They weren't millionaire kids but had facilities for swimming, horse riding, squash, tennis and golf.
- They knew by heart all epaulettes and can figure out an officer's rank correctly.
- They clearly knew which CSD canteen had which stock is stacked in which corner.
- Their vacations were a package deal consisting of form D, Army Jonga and mess guest room.
- B'day bashes comprised of all age-group children and at times even pets in tow!
- Only they knew what 'pagal gymkhana' was assorted games!
- Their house had stuff from all parts of the country.
- Every house had a settee - made out of condemned ammo cartons, a sarkari black blanket and an old embroidered cloth.
- ... and finally when Papa retired it took Mom about 12 years to get rid of the *kabaar* that had been accumulated/ hoarded over the years. It include - about 30 to 40 wooden boxes all painted black; 3 boxes of Precis/Pamphlets from YO's Course to DSSC; two boxes full of shoes and Web equipment of all hues; plenty of brass mementoes which looked like knights on horses; old cannons or some sort of imaginary work of modern art which looked more like flashes of lightning (the concept of which only Papa could explain after two drinks!!); few empty brass cartridges, which used to be brassoed every time we had someone visiting our house; two sets of Naga spears; five types of

dahs; two khukris; one Mizo bow and about 20 arrows; fishing rods (the hooks had been hidden by Mom long ago lest some brat managed to get them inserted into his hand or eye!!); four machchardanis and 16 rods/bamboo sticks; one World War II helmet; one parachute; one High Alti Parkas; Papa's 18 pairs of shoes; one shiny green Coloured Great Coat; ten fungus-eaten leather belts; moth-eaten OG pullovers and balaclavas; one High Alti sleeping bag; key chains made out of M14 anti-personnel mine safety clips; one Pack 08 and about four FS packs; Web belts; one pistol holster; one cowboy hat; one Barah Bore Bandook; one .32 pistol; possibly one Springfield rifle (whose ammo is no more available and has become a nuisance to get rid of !!); four daggers; about five walking sticks; two sarkari canes; one swagger stick; one chabuk!; one leather crossbelt; about five whistles; thirty metres of hassain cloth in various stages of decomposition, having been recycled during various transfers!; about 80 kg of drift wood; almost 400 white coloured stones that were picked up from some god-forsaken river bed in Sikkim to be used one day for landscaping of the garden after retirement; 60 to 70 flower pots; 100 metres of water pipes (in bits and pieces); one unused fish aquarium; 50 metres of cable WD, old Blanco cakes; one folding camp cot; one folding camp chair which has the nasty habit of injuring the hands of any inexperienced person trying to open it; two *Namdas,* about four to six rusted dog leashes still attached to rotting dog Collars; not to forget the *jhoola* that was made long ago after taking lot of obligations of the 'Workshop Uncle'; and paintings, not of MF Husain type but yet famous Kalimpong products.

Though I have described the above paraphernalia as *kabar*, Fauji kids are proud of what they got and what they have and are aware of the sacrifices the parents made, toiling honestly and with fullest integrity. A culture apart, which millions of Indians would want to experience and are highly envious about.

Moulding the Officer's Wife into Army Life

A college going girl whose daily life revolves around getting her mobile recharged to arguing with the rickshaw puller for the money charged or even grabbing a quick bite at one of the suburbian eating joint. She by getting married to an Army officer, her life transforms quickly into a lady who knows her manners and etiquettes till the very bottom of the line and thereby she carries herself with utmost grace and pinache in other's presence. The army is one establishment where one's social etiquette is honed to perfection. At the base of it all is the cardinal attribute of humility, which one learns due to the system of hierarchy.

The army officer's wife gradually learns many creative arts because at every new location she begins with setting up her accommodation in tune with the city. Without exception every Army officer's wife knows flora and fauna. Courtesy various ladies meet they learn flower arrangement, singing, choreography and grow in confidence by conducting few events. At times life becomes difficult and lonely when they get posted to small station/field area. Over here, one has to live in a bashas (a makeshift arrangement) with only two/three families close by. This opportunity is also taken as a challenge and the families make most of these tenures by learning from each other.

For an Army wife, a teaching job with suitable hours is all right. This way they can attend to their family as well as fulfill the obligations of Army life. The social commitments as an Army wife are all encompassing but can be profoundly satisfying depending on positive outlook. On the other side of cozy Army family life are times when loneliness stretches over when one's husband is away on a temporary duty or exercise. During this period of seperation all the ladies rally around each other as family. Anything which suffers in the bargain is that of children's education.

Army officer's wife grow up to be a responsible and matured lady as she often dons the role of "double parenting". This way she learns to cope with all; because the smallest and most important unit in society - the family - gets to spend more qualitative time together. "One becomes an enlightened personality by learning to live in all kinds of situations".

World Apart from Civvie Street Job

Quality of life is an important facet of the Army career and it has no parallel in any other government or PSU service. The Indian Army provides you a status of Class I officer at an early age of 21! What else one wants? Quality of Army life is beyond the civilian's imagination. On the civvie street, a job with a thick pay packet comes with a heavy baggage - a mundane 9 am to 9 pm or beyond schedule, no time for extra-curricular activities, no chance for adventurous activities and challenges, no social recognition, and uncertainty of pink slip with a month's salary. In contrast, the Indian Army job offers excitement, adventure, thrill, honour, prestige, self-esteem, safety and job security for the family. And, above all, one command the love and respect of all the citizens of the country. In the prevailing uncertain social and economic conditions the worldwide, Army as a profession is an island of sanity and social order that is the envy of all countrymen. Some of the intangibles, which define the quality of life in the Army, are:

- Serve the country with honour, self-respect and dignity.
- Travel worldwide and gain first-hand experience on all aspects of life.
- Gain exposure of the cultures of various countries by being part of the United Nations Peacekeeping Missions.
- Noble profession which is ranked the best.
- Profession of high social acceptability.

- Remain rejuvenated throughout as one posting is for two years.
- Ample scope for development both on professional and personal fronts.
- Sports and adventure activities.
- Education facilities - Both school and professional Colleges for children.
- AWWA hostels for girls in metros.
- Prompt medical attention.
- Quality of life ensured not only for officers but also for their families.

Variety and Adventures

Variety and adventure are the spice and romance of life. No profession has the kind of recreational and adventure facilities to offer as the Army - from membership of the best clubs in the country to horse riding, swimming, golfing, mountaineering, trekking and sailing. Posting to exotic stations gives one an opportunity to see India and its different cultures in all their vivid glory. One also gets a chance to go abroad on course or on posting. So, if one is looking for a profession which goes beyond being a mere job, one must accept the challenge and join the Indian Army.

Professional Enhancement

The Army affords a very open, impartial and transparent avenue for professional enhancement. For a professionally dedicated officer with sincerity and dedication, the sky is the limit for professional enhancement. Salient aspects of professional enhancement in the Army are as follows:

(a) Opportunity for higher study in prestigious institutions both in India and abroad.

(b) Deputation in various scientific institutions in the country including DRDO, DGQA, BEL, IIT and a host of others.

(c) Foreign assignments in the UNO and Indian embassies/ missions.

(d) Foreign assignments in connection with the procurement of advanced technology and weaponry and training to handle and maintain the same.

(e) Promotions solely based on capability and free of any extraneous considerations.

Second Career

Generally, it is perceived that servicemen face difficulties when they leave Armed forces, especially in the present competitive environment. But they have an inherent advantage in the job market. On scrutinising a CV listing Army experience and qualifications, prospective employers find it interesting and motivating. Mainly they say: "Your CV is impressive. You've worked for the same employer for 25 years — a testament to your loyalty, and you've demonstrated a commitment to your career, not just a job."

With enriched experience, finding a job outside of the Forces should be a relatively easy progression - as long as one moves positively. Employers in the commercial sector recognise the experience and qualifications a soldier brings along, although acquired in a different context. Technical skills aside, soldiers bring loyalty, discipline and fantastic teamwork skills - all fundamental traits that are essential to a successful team.

I have spent more than two years in the corporate world and let me confess that life of an Indian Army officer is in true sense full of challenges. The ecstatic feeling of commanding the troops, adventure activities and living on the edge in operational areas makes life fulfilling. It is an experience of a rarest kind. Each youth should take this opportunity even by joining through a short service commission for 5 years and then go for a second career.

Man Management

IIMs can count on the Indian Army for case studies when it comes to man management. Undeniably, the Indian Army's man management is par excellence. Junior officers lead from the front, and that's why soldiers follow their officers through a hail of shrapnel and bullets. On the face of it, it may seem outrageous but in reality it happens in routine. It is because men look up to their officers with awe and respect for their personal care and touch. In fact, for officers and men the relationship is like that of a family, and the bonding is much stronger than their own family as they brave heat, cold, hail and bullets together. Officers spend quality time with their men by attending to their personal and professional issues. The bonding is of a very special kind and it puts the Indian Army on a high pedestal.

Military Life vs. Civilian Life

Military life is a life of challenges much beyond the comprehension of civilians.

- A soldier remains awake for many nights at a stretch because of his duty on borders or even during exercises.
- Goes without proper meal for many days when he is out on a long patrol duty or on operational duty.
- No contact with his family at times for months if posted at a place where there is no connectivity of his mobile phone.
- He goes without a bath for few months when posted at Siachen Glacier or at high altitude.
- No wearing of fancy clothes for many months as long as he remains on duty.
- Proceeds on leave almost all the times without a proper train reservation.
- Diwali, Holi and all major festivals are mainly celebrated away from his kith and kin.

- The soldier never questions why. He lays down his life for the country smilingly.

During field duty, the soldier eats food in mestin, drinks water from natural sources, dons his olive green uniform most of the time and sleeps in the bunker.

Life of Turbulences and Turmoils

Life's turbulences and turmoils have a special meaning for the soldier which is beyond the understanding of a common man. For a soldier, the spectrum of threat ranges from the conventional war to counter-insurgency operations, with terrorism emerging like a hydra-headed monster. Coupled to it are the vagaries of terrain and climate of the Siachen Glacier and other glacial heights and extreme cold, dense mountainous forests and the heat of the desert. The soldier smilingly operates under these trying conditions for better future of the Nation. He often goes beyond the call of duty. The soldier is imbibed by a set of ethics that makes him willingly lay down his life for the nation. Supreme sacrifice! The values of the Army as an institution are deeply rooted in all soldiers. These are:

- **Camaraderie:** The values of comradeship and espirit de corps of the gallant, regardless of caste, sex or religion. Essence of camaraderie is "one for all and all for one".
- **Supreme Sacrifice:** The soldier follows the age-old adage: Not to question why, but to do or die for the three "Ns" - Naam, that is, name or honour of the unit/Army/nation; Namak (salt), that is, loyalty to the nation; and Nishan, that is, the insignia or flag of his unit/regiment/Army/nation which jawans hold with immense pride. Soldiers willingly do supreme sacrifice.
- **Veerta Aur Vivek:** No sign of fear whatsoever be the situation. Maintain a calm and composed demeanour under trying and challenging situations.
- **Apolitical:** The Indian Army does not discriminate on account of caste, creed or religion. A soldier is a soldier first and anything else later. He prays under a common

roof with fellow soliders. It is this unique character, which makes him bind in a team despite coming from a different background.

- **Fairness and Honesty:** The soldier fights for a just cause that extends even to the enemy (prisoner or wounded).
- **Discipline and Integrity:** Discipline and integrity impart to the soldier the feeling of patriotism, honesty and courage under all circumstances, however strong be the provocation.
- **Honour and Courage:** The soldier is a man on whose shoulders lie the honour and integrity of his nation. He knows that he is the last line of defence and he cannot fail the nation.
- **Death to Dishonour:** The greatest binding force in the Indian Army remains unit cohesion and tradition. Truly heady is this mixture of unit identification and traditions of sacrificial valour, handed down through centuries. At one point, victory or defeat becomes irrelevant. What matters is – Has the unit measured up to the occasion? A close bond among soldiers makes them to choose death over dishonour. The concept of *izzat* (honour) in the clan/unit enables them to shun the fear of death. For them; to be called a coward in the peer group is worse than death.
- **Forthrightness:** The soldier has to be forthright, for on his word the men he leads are going to lay down their lives without questioning why.

These values stoke the attitude of 'Service before Self' in every soldier. The famous credo of Chetwode Hall is deeply imbibed by the men in olive green. It is the spirit of this credo that binds every officer with his men in an unshakable bond of camaraderie.

Do you have it in you?

The above heading represents a common saying, rather a question, which has now rightly been associated with the Indian Army. The Army life is demanding. For a soldier, normal family life is a dream. Yet, you command men who display a high degree of loyalty and follow the quote "Not to question why, but to do or die". Such is the charm of the profession of soldiering that a person can endure hardships and even death without murmur or crib.

You think you have it in you to lead the country and provide a backbone for it? You think it is your responsibility to protect your motherland and its countrymen? Do you have the guts and the drive to live on the edge and face the world as it is? Well then, the Indian Army is your calling. The Indian Army is the second largest standing Army in the world with around 11,00,000 active and 9,60,000 reserve soldiers. Their main motive is to ensure national security and defend the country against other forces which also include terrorists. The army is also deployed for helping the victims of natural calamities such as floods, earthquakes and landslides. Being in the Indian Army is one of the most adventurous, challenging and prestigious position anyone can ever dream of. It allows you to have a privileged lifestyle with some of the best perks anyone could ever dream of while at the same time determines and builds your character.

To join the Army, before looking into the eligibility factors, you need to realize as to whether you have a strong will power and can actually face the challenges ahead of you, knowing the fact that you have to give up pretty much everything. Putting this in more stringent words, it implies giving up on your own lifestyle.

Well then, if you want to fulfil your childhood dreams of saluting the Indian flag and take pride in wearing the military uniform, while people would look at you with awe, go and leave a mark for yourself and the country.

Then,
"Join Indian Army"

CHAPTER 2

Down the Memory Lane

I felt elated to be among the few who had been privileged to make it to the prestigious National Defence Academy (NDA) after class XIIth in the year 1984. There is so much to write, but again so much which has to be censored by me lest youngsters get intimidated by the hard work that is synonymous with the NDA. One's three-year stay is the best one can think of in one's lifetime.

It's an odd feeling now when I reminisce the ostensibly "hard-to-get-over" three years at the NDA. What a big transformation I underwent - in personality, thinking, outlook towards life, physical structure, positive attitude et al. The NDA training consisted of six terms. The first term training was conducted at NDA wing at Ghorpuri. Each of the six terms came with new privileges (within the squadron), new opportunities, new competitions, "new headaches," new responsibilities and, of course, "added respect". To help cadets out, there are various kinds of "pal-funda" – "name-type pals," "place-type pals," "b'day-type pals," "school-type-pals"... You name a common factor and approach and build rapport with a senior to experience "uplift" whenever you are facing predicaments during training.

Ridding You of the Ego Baggage

The first day of the second term was very jittery. I had no idea what I was stepping into. I joined **Bravo Squadron**. Within 24 hours, life was in a spin, and the spinning wheel had no friction! The first phase of the second term consists of breaking the inherent ego that is in the minds of guys coming from Class XII. The best part is it is not done by slapping or manhandling. A few "cream-rolls" here (read rolling on the undulating ground), a few back rolls there, and you come to the ground level. You "unlearn" everything that you have brought to the Academy. And, you are ready to become an officer endowed with qualities to be among the top-notch in whatever field you would be.

There was so much to do – PT, running, breakfast (an event per se), classes, clubs, games, "moving in" (i.e. doing zillions of push-ups to enter the squadron) after the games, study period, dinner, and post-dinner activities. Thankfully wearing a wrist-watch was a sixth term privilege...used to just wait and wait and wait for time to pass by... No dearth of activities – riding, polo, swimming, mountain climbing, sailing, golf, photography, firing et al.

For all the terms, every day was a new day. It was like somehow doing all the activities and making it to your bed safe and sound at night. Going from squadron for breakfast, breakfast to classes, going from one LH (lecture hall) to another, classes to lunch and onwards, without getting caught by appointments, lifting up bicycles, running around poles et al was a big deal!!

The camps were tough, made us tougher - mentally and physically. The camp life helped us imbibe the spirit of "Never give up" and "There is no limit to human endurance... none at all!!".

Following a candidate's selection in one of the three Services - Army, Navy and Air Force, he is given preliminary training, both academic and physical, for a period of three years at the NDA. The training during the first two and a half years is common to the cadets of the three wings. The three years' training at the NDA leads to a graduate degree (BA, BSc or BSc in Computer Science) awarded by Jawaharlal Nehru University, New Delhi.

On passing out from the NDA, Army cadets go to the Indian Military Academy (IMA), Dehradun, Naval cadets to INS Cochin, the Cadets' Training Ship, and Air Force cadets to the Air Force Academy, Hyderabad.

Gentleman Cadet

The Indian Military Academy (IMA) is an integral part of the Dehradun landscape. One cannot imagine the Doon Valley without the **Chetwode Building**, which is the heart and soul of the IMA. This historic building adds a unique glory to the city and makes it proud of the several generations of young men who have passed out as officers from the IMA and served the nation excellently. It would be interesting to note that maximum number of Army officers' wives hail from Dehradun. At the IMA, an army cadet is known as Gentleman Cadet (GC). The Gentleman Cadets (GCs) become an integral but special part of Dehradun's ambience when they are out in the markets and streets, relaxing on their days off. They are the reason for many young girls and boys to join the elite force.

The IMA was inaugurated formally by Field Marshal Sir Philip Chetwode on December 10, 1932. The Chetwode Building is named after Sir Philip Chetwode. At the IMA, GCs are given strenuous military training for a period of one year or year and half to transform them into officers capable of leading Infantry sub-units. The training emphasis is on instilling a sense of responsibility through a fit body and robust mind. After undergoing the organised and systematic IMA training, you never think a problem is too big. You break it down into smaller parts and address each with one thought – to reach the logical end. The benefit is that you stay in the present and move forward, instead of being rooted in thought. On successful completion of the IMA training, the cadets are granted a Permanent Commission.

The IMA has set up a Honour Code Committee. The **Honour Code** commands GCs to adhere to the value system of integrity, loyalty and moral courage. And, violators of the code are punished based on the GC's own committee. This way one learns to take tough decisions dispassionately.

The **'buddy system'** at the IMA instils the highly desired and appreciated quality of selflessness among GCs. They learn to protect their mates before themselves in true spirit of the Chetwode saying or credo of the Academy: **"The safety, honour and welfare of your country come first, always and every time. The honour, welfare and comfort of the men you command come next. Your own ease, comfort and safety come last, always and every time."** These historic words, inscribed in letters of gold inside the Chetwode Hall, are famously quoted by all military leaders. This also formed part of the Chetwode inaugural address. The Chetwode saying echoes in the heart of every officer of the Indian Army all his life after leaving the IMA.

The Motto

IMA's motto is ***Veerta aur Vivek*** (Valour and Wisdom) and its Colours are steel grey and red – the first for resilience and the second signifying the ultimate sacrifice in the service of the nation. After successfully completing training at IMA, with pride I can say that I got commissioned into the regiment of my choice and in the regiment I was fortunate enough to get commissioned in the Kali Chindi battalion which had a cherished history.

Life in Infantry Battalion

- Getting bored with the civilian life, I saw the Army as a challenge. I wanted to measure up to that challenge and push myself and be pushed by my superiors everyday so that I could not only better myself and achieve my own personal goals, but I could also bring my battalion closer to achieving its goals.
- I chose the Infantry over other options because of the opportunity for advancement and the abundance of training to help me become one of the best.
- I understood that there would be long periods of boredom, but I would need to always maintain my focused "go-getter" attitude. But being a member of an Infantry battalion, I had more motivation to do everything and anything.
- Infantry is physically intense. Everyday physical training made me tough and fit physically.
- Wanted to feel like a member of a team in a brotherhood, which has purpose and goals. Everything that is done in the military, no matter how large or small, has a purpose.
- I performed well in the mandatory courses including the commando course. My routine in the Infantry battalion was an extension of training days at the NDA and IMA. Right from attending PT in the morning to checking guards in the night, one remained closely associated with the troops from whom one learnt a lot on a daily basis. Soon, I was entrusted upon with the staff responsibilities. In a nutshell, all was going well as any YO (young officer) would desire.
- Volunteered to do para jumps as a GC from the IMA itself during the summer break of the second term.

Undertook military operations under extreme difficult and risky situations. Even after having applied for premature retirement (PMR), I requested for field posting in the operational Northern Command.

Regimental System

The core of the Army fabric is the regimental system, which grooms young officers into leaders of men. The values and ethos instilled by the regimental system into the young officers transform them from ordinary youth into extraordinary leaders of men. There are no formal classes that help bring this transformation. It is achieved through spending formative years in the unit going through the grind with the men, with continued guidance by senior officers through words and by setting personal examples.

The regimental system assumes importance in the Infantry life because an Infantry officer remains in pickets perched on hilltops for two or three years in inhospitable terrains without electricity and basic facilities. The regimental system that we have followed so long has been our biggest strength in the battlefield. I have also often noticed that the regimental ties tend to become thicker with each passing day of military career.

Nostalgia!!!

I look back at my Army career with pride and content and would like to join an Infantry battalion in my next birth. It was a fulfilling and rewarding career in true sense of the words. But as there are two sides of everything, so is the case with my Army career. It came to an unplanned end due to unprofessional behaviour of certain quarters in the Army for a soldier like me who was and is still professional to the core. The following statutory and non-statutory complaints, filed by me with appropriate authorities in the Army, will give you an idea of what led to my premature retirement (PMR) from the Army, a profession which has brought out a paradigm shift in my personality.

At the fag end of my career I submitted a statutory complaint which will provide readers an insight into how non-professional issue takes precedence over professional competence. It reads:

Statutory Complaint

1. **Main Points of the Complaint:**

(a) My statutory complaint is a sequel to my non-statutory complaint dated 17 Nov 2005 submitted against non-empanelment.

(b) In my last five reports, I have been continuously rated outstanding. In spite of being non-empanelled, the report earned on 20 April 2006 clearly states that the officer takes pride in his profession. I will continue to do so but alongside put across my representation.

(c) In succeeding paragraphs, I once again would like to highlight certain key issues. These are mainly FRESH FACTS:

(i) **Advisory Remark:** The whole ACR (Annual Confidential Report) hinges around one non-professional issue, i.e. family discord. Be it as it is, still it is an advisory remark. Even the language of the pen picture is advisory in nature as it reads: "Officer should learn to keep his family discord within four walls". I would like to draw attention to letter No. 044791/MS: Policy dated 21 October 1998. The letter may kindly be scrutinised so as to draw relevant deductions. I only wish to highlight that an advisory remark if acted upon seriously by the ratee and doesn't find mention in subsequent reports, then, accordingly it should be vetted/analysed. The very fact that such a remark has never been endorsed again or was never reflected ever, hence it should be treated solely as an advisory remark. I would also like to mention that later on during an informal get-together, Brig KN Mehra (who initiated this ACR) himself admitted that initially on my non-statutory complaint dated 16 September 2000 he endorsed strong comments to justify his reporting against the family discord but later on, he himself with passage of time (over three years) forwarded comments to my statutory complaint dated 28 November 2003 in such a manner so as to provide with an opportunity to get due redress. By stating these two facts, i.e. never an advisory remark has been endorsed in my ACR and even the officer who reflected this remark had later presumably softened his stance goes to prove that this was merely an advisory remark.

(ii) **Ignorance:** At times in my sombre mood, I am compelled to think that had I not represented against this ACR, I stood a fair chance of getting it expunged on its own merit during internal assessment. I committed the cardinal mistake of submitting a non-statutory complaint. Obviously, the reviewing officer stood his ground by commenting upon it in a harsh manner. Although later, with the passage of time, i.e. more than three years, his comments had softened up. Hence, once again on non-empanelment the ACR in question met the same fate. Therefore, my request is that the ACR be viewed de novo against my overall career profile and the initial comments be viewed against the comments of the same reporting officer which he endorsed later on in my statutory complaint (28 November 2003).

(iii) **Well Corroborated Reporting:** I am more than confident that beside this report all my other reports must have been either outstanding/near outstanding as I was always appreciated by my seniors for my professional competence. Since the rejection order reads that it's well corroborated, hence it makes me think that in the impugned ACR, the SRO would have also replicated what RO had endorsed. Therefore, I wish to draw attention to the DO letter dated 29 April 2000 attached with my statutory complaint of 28 November 2003. I received no reply to this letter of mine. The very fact that he accepted my thanks-giving letter, made me always feel that he would have set the records straight. Sadly and unfortunately, now it doesn't seem to be true. As stated in my non-statutory complaint dated 17 November 2005 I made the SRO aware of the happenings at SFF Academy. Further, as stated by him and mentioned by me in the above mentioned DO letter under reference, I was under the impression that the needful would have been done by the SRO. He retired on 31 July 2000 and probably never commented upon my non-statutory complaint. Therefore, all throughout it is one reporting officer's comment against my representation.

(iv) **Reckonable Period:** The order reads that the impugned ACR is in tune with my overall profile in the reckonable period. I sincerely hope that as stated, the impugned ACR is viewed against all my reports from nine-year service onwards (reckonable period). Still, not leaving anything to chance, I would like to mention that the ACR I earned in the year 1993 was set aside on its own owing to IO's subjective reporting and that's the reason I withdrew my stat complaint dated 01 September 1995. I was informed about the expunction of remarks (MS Branch letter No. 660107/1490/MS-4C) by Lt Col NPS Hira, AMS Southern Command in January 1996.

(v) **Career Profile:** Barring the impugned ACR, all my ACRs are either outstanding or near outstanding and most of the ACRs have been earned in operational areas. On the contrary, the impugned ACR has been earned on an ERE tenure. Further, all my course gradings are also well above average. I have done reasonably well at Defence Services Staff College, Wellington and that's the reason I was posted as GSO 2 (Ops) of a RR Sector. Also, I have been decorated in an operational area for killing a terrorist.

(vi) **Adequately Exercised Period:** The reports earned by me as a Company Commander are in operational areas (Intense Counter Insurgency Operations). The reports earned may kindly be seen (2001 and 2003) and appropriate objective analysis be drawn. With all humbleness I would like to submit that planting a mole in a terrorist organisation is a unique feat and in all probability an unparallel achievement in the Indian Army history. To my bad luck, this report of May 2003 by MS-4 has been enfaced as inflated. What's my fault! If possible, before brushing aside this report, it is requested that the letter written by my IO, Col NK Raja (who had initiated the ACR), as well as the reply by Col MS-4 may kindly be scrutinised because my CO had objected to the enfacement of this ACR 'inflated'.

(vii) **Family Discord:** I had explicitly mentioned the circumstances under which this remark was endorsed in my non-stat complaint. Besides all reporting officers, more than two General officers also have reported positively on my marital status. As late as 21 Jun '06, none other than present DGMO Lt Gen Mohan Pande in writing mentioned highly about my maturity, commitment and professional competence. Self and my wife are deeply religious. We observe two fasts a week and I also observed Roza fasts with my troops in Nov-Dec. 2000. Mine is a family which plays and prays together. Being a teetotaller and a strict vegetarian, I understand family values. In my report of May 2001, it has been written that I am a devoted father to my daughters. My non-empanelment on this issue of family discord will have a far reaching effect on my two grown-up daughters. Further, my wife has been Principal of Army Schools for the last three years and has contributed immensely. The very fact that we still stay happily together goes to prove that my priorities are in right place and I do not place advancement in career ahead of family.

(viii) **Biased Reporting:** Right from the first complaint onwards, I am giving out the reasons for biased reporting. This belief of mine further gets substantiated when I recently learnt that the other officer who took up interview with the RO against Officiating

Cdr [mentioned in my non-stat complaint dated 16 September 2000 at Para 1 (e)] was also fixed by the RO. Further, I gave an account of high degree of honesty and integrity (Refer Para 2 (d) (iv) of non-statutory complaint dated 16 September 2000) but still I was graded with 7 marks in integrity. Undoubtedly, the whole ACR was initiated with a biased and prejudiced mind and in a manner that I stand no chance of redress (one six, sevens in all asterisks qualities and sprinkling of eights). Thereby, the report gets well corroborated. As stated earlier, there was no verbal warning and had the family discord been so grave and serious why was I given permission to stay with family in field area (permission to stay with family was given on three months basis by the Commandant). I continued to stay with the family right till the end of the tenure. Further if the family discord was so apparent and demeaning, why was I not given a written warning. I once again humbly mention that in order to put me on defensive, the family discord was made an issue so as to divert my attention from the main issue of irregularities in tender action of 04 October 1999. I could have also sensed the timing of it and would have kept quiet. But this was not to be. I continued to put across the impropriety on the part of Lt Col Pankaj Awasthi right from day one. How do I prove myself? As per the format, I am rendering a certificate that any false accusation should render me liable for disciplinary action. My humble plea is that kindly investigate thoroughly and properly into the circumstances and the blemish of family discord be removed.

(ix) **Aberration:** I have earned reports before and after this impugned ACR. The reports earned are in difficult and challenging environment and have been reported upon by mainly different reporting officers. The impugned CR has been damaged at the behest of Lt Col Pankaj Awasthi, SM*** whose credentials were always under the scanner. He is son-in-law of the infamous Maj Gen Gupta who ran away from the train while being brought from Chennai for investigation against his misdeeds in IPKF and later surfaced up after three years to fetch his pension. Col Pankaj Awasthi has also recently retired from service.

(x) **Justice:** I had put across my representations with an open mind as well as unmindful of the repercussions and outcome. Since my first non-stat complaint dated 16 September 2000 against the impugned ACR, I have been highlighting the misdemeanour and impropriety on the part of Lt Col Pankaj Awasthi, the Officiating Cdr of SFF Academy. To this effect, as per format, I tender a certificate that any false accusation should render me liable for disciplinary action. The rejection order of non-statutory complaint dated 18 November '05 states: "Giving details of tender action for procurement of rock climbing stores, he has cited certain irregularities[1] in the issue and the role of the Officiating Commander in the matter. He has stated that the tough stand taken by him in writing about its incorrectness led to cancellation of the tender action. He adds that as the Officiating Commander was close to the Comdt (RO), a small issue was projected as a family discord in his case to put him, the complainant, on the defensive. As he had put the issues related to the tender action down in writing, the same did not go down well with the senior officers and they probably decided to fix him through the tool of CRs". Unlike, court of law, no provision exists for putting across counter affidavits. I do not know what is going against me and I am not getting redress for one aberrative report. I am of the firm opinion (as stated in rejection order of non-statutory complaint) my this report is definitely not in tune with my other reports in reckonable period. Therefore, once again, I sincerely pray that this impugned CR be viewed de novo in the light of the circumstances in which it was initiated and my overall career profile (till date) and especially against the backdrop of my performance in operational areas.

1 **Gross Injustice**! The Army continued to keep its eyes closed in spite of bringing out financial irregularities by me and also in spite of rendering a certificate of correctness.

(d) **Representation:** My one report based on reasons beyond the realms of professional competence has sealed my career. I have continued to represent as I am optimistic that finally one day justice will prevail and I will get my due. This being my last chance within the organisation for redress, I may have overstepped and would have brought out something which otherwise I would have vetted. But, this should be understood from someone's point of view who has strived hard (Above average course reports, Staff College, killed terrorists in both the Company Commander tenures, risked life to plant mole in a terrorist organisation, as a BM also officiated as DQ and DAAG and continuously being rated outstanding in last many reports). Since my first non-statutory complaint dated 16 September 2000 (Refer Para 1 (n) of non-statutory complaint) I am maintaining my stance that I may be called upon anytime to further substantiate[2] any statement.

2. **Redressal Sought:**
   (a) CR of 2000 be expunged in its entirety.
   (b) Any aberration in my career profile be expunged.

3. **Supporting Documents Attached:** Nil

4. **Certificate:** I undertake that any false accusation or false statement made by me in this complaint will render me liable for disciplinary action.

Over the entire army career spanning over more than two decades I had put across my grievances regularly but to no avail. Gist of my other complaints are enumerated as under:

Gist of all my complaints till date

Non-Stat Complaint of 11 March 1994

- As per the rules no channel can withhold such a complaint unless a redress has been given to the

2 **Substantial Proof.** Ample evidence was there to pinpoint misuse of funds.

satisfaction of the complainant. The complaint has to be forwarded within the next ten days, along with the intermediate Commanders' comments. This is the procedure and has been followed a number of times by different officers.

- Whereas my complaint of March '94, when submitted to Col VK Singh, he conveniently forwarded it to HQ 114 Inf Bde where I was to move out because he did not want his chain of command to know his deeds (I had attached the DO letter dated 16 January '94) as his ACR was due and he was to move for HC. Again, I submitted complaint against this ACR from 24 Rajput wherein I brought out the misuse of MCN. This time I was asked by my CO to withdraw it because the ACR has been expunged owing to its subjectivity. But the question remains why no note was taken of the misuse of MCN. It's a court martial offence and an officer of 61 CAVALRY was courtmartialled for its misuse, herein, Col VK Singh commits a grave offence, not only gets away with it in spite of this being brought to the notice of senior officers but also rises to the rank of COAS with this integrity traits.

The question, therefore, in all fairness must be examined so that:

- Justice not only is served but is also seen to be served.
- Action is taken so that the interests of the service are not allowed to suffer.
- Action is taken so that such incidents do not reoccur.

Highlights of Non-Stat Complaint of 16 Sept 2000

- **Integrity:** Brought down rate of eqpt purchased by nearly 50% to save exchequer lakhs of rupees
- **Stuck my neck out:** Wrote two confidential letters[3] dated 18 November '99 and 13 December '99 to Lt Col Pankaj Awasthi, Offg Cdr to make my stand clear against impropriety.

---

3 **Arbitrariness.** What else! Did it not warrant a thorough probe into procurement process.

- **Deprivation of bona fide Duty:** Violation/ infringement of AO 7/95, wherein after having initiated the ACRs someone else rewrote it for troops under my command.
- **Result:** No investigation.

Highlights of Statutory Complaint of 28 Nov 2003

Asked for ACR to be viewed de novo.

Adverse remark: Remarks of RO which led to filing of complaint were toned down after a gap of nearly four years.

- **Result:** No relief.

Non-statutory Complaint of 18 Nov 2005 on Non-Empanelment

Redress Sought: I wrote strongly that to vindicate my stand against impropriety ACR be set aside.

- **Result:** No redressal.

The way complaints were handled showed that one's performance and integrity has no bearing on the ACR. You can scream from the top of South Block but it will not have any echo effect on the hallowed corridors of South Block. If you've stepped out of the line to comment upon then God save you or how else all impropriety questions weren't answered!

Inferences

Regarding my final statutory complaint (page 39), the following inferences are obvious:

Impropriety: If the system is transparent and accountable then why was I not asked to substantiate my statement wherein I brought out malpractices.

- **Professionalism:** Does a non-professional issue play a predominant role in a soldier's career!
- **Allahabad HC Ruling:** Did my move to Allahabad HC antagonize people in the Army and there itself was it decided that I be treated as an outcast!

- **Apprehension:** That if an outspoken and no-nonsense officer like me makes it to the next rank (Colonel) it will lay bare more unscrupulous activities of senior ranking officer.

From the very beginning I knew that if I state that my stand be vindicated, my redressal will not see the light of the day. I still went ahead with it so as to ensure that the vetting officer reads it in the right perspective. It is intriguing to note that in spite of my stance since 2000 no one ever felt to investigate the circumstances under which the purchases was made. Least, while making note on redressal it could have been mentioned that the subject matter was inquired into and after ascertaining all related issues/facts no redressal is given. This never happens! Reasons best known to the Army and MOD!!

Even, earlier when I commented on misuse of MCN (Military Credit Note) in statutory complaint of '94, no action was initiated. **Fait accompli**! In spite of repeated indifferent response, I continued with my duty so as to continually maintain my honour in front of my troops. The two command reports which I earned are reproduced here:

Report earned at Poonch Sector (Year 1999-2000)

Arun is an intelligent officer with an analytical mind, who is very highly motivated and task-oriented. He is held in very high esteem by his peers and subordinates for his professional competence, espirit-de-corps, enthusiasm and team spirit. He has a very good sense of humour and remains balanced in challenging sit. The officer commanded his coy very effectively in CI ops in very rugged high attitude trn in Poonch district of JandK. He personally led an op which resulted in the elimination of a foreign mercenary and a guide, demonstrating great courage during the encounter. He also used his initiative and ingenuity to construct a realistic combat range which greatly improved the battle reflexes of his men. He kept his soldiers motivated and cheerful in a very challenging environment. He willingly shoulders additional responsibilities and puts in his best efforts to the assigned tasks. The officer is happily married and is a devoted father to his two pretty daughters. He has been nominated to attend the DSSC which is a result of his perseverance and sustained efforts to achieve professional excellence.

Report earned at Anantnag Sector (Year 2002-2003)

Arun is an exceptionally brilliant and highly spirited officer who cheerfully leads his tps by pers example from the front - even in the most hostile and critical sits. The officer possesses an uncanny knack for turning defeat into victory and a victory into a spectacular landmark event. The immense care of his men that he takes, and the ability to turn grim faces smiling makes him an instant choice, as a ldr.

Having joined the unit as a rif coy cdr in OP PARAKRAM, at a very critical phase in a sensitive op sect, with an acutely low officer str in the unit - Arun shouldered the addl responsibilities as the Offg 2IC and contributed most immensely in the unit's training as 2nd in command more noticeably bringing out a paradigm change in the rock–craft trg skills by getting on with the nuts and bolts of the op - plan at unit and sub-unit level in a realistic trn. In the subsequent emp of the unit for CT ops, he not only evolved a superb int network but also succeeded in making an active terrorist, as own source, leading to total breakdown of terrorist str and ops in the AOR. He has personally led a No. of successful ops, facing bullets and silencing the terrorists - most notably that of the killing of most wanted for 13 yrs, the HM dist cdr of Anantnag with his trusted aide. Thereafter, in the mega-event of Amarnath Yatra and the historic JandK elections, Arun worked tirelessly to ensure a zero-incident pd on the most IED (Improvised Explosive Device) prone rd in the corps Z and also ensured an overwhelmingly successful and enthusiastic people's participation in sensitive star-constituency of Bijbehare and Pehalgam.

Arun has displayed a very high degree of maturity and well balanced considerate approach in dealing with subordinates, colleagues and superiors. He is a live-wire in the unit and is at the forefront of stn / fmn activities and is loyal to the core to the org. His ability to conceptualise a theme in a given environment, critically analyse the obj/ key factors and judiciously utilise the available/created resources - makes him a winner. The officer is happily married and the couple has impeccable social manner and sense of responsibility.

Matter of Pride

It needs to be stated that physical courage in battle is not something which can be taken for granted for any group of men. There are some men who do very well and very few who fail. The bulk of the group performs depending mainly on the junior leader's actions. Since he is himself exposed to the same risks, he has to set the example. Some individuals buckle under the awesome strain. It is the supreme test of combat leadership, which, if found wanting, leads to disaster. All men feel fear, but some succumb completely under stress. With repeated exposure, troops and junior leaders develop a close understanding of the effects of fire and to an extent overcome their individual fears.

I performed under exceptional circumstances and would have carried on with same daring leadership skills. One may list one's contribution to the Army career as:

- Killing terrorist - epitome of soldierly qualities.
- Have performed well on courses, thereby knowing military craft well.
- Got the team trained to win a professional competition at the highest level.

- Served as a true leader – Soldiers vouch for!
- Lived under the shadow of death every moment of the day in a hostile environment and ensured that the troops under my command suffered no causalities.
- Conducted above board especially in financial matters.
- Qualified for competitive exam with good grades.

But one's own response to this contribution listing could be: So what? Tangible contributions are to be acknowledged. Intangibles such as sycophancy and turning a blind eye to seniors' misdeeds are prerequisites to satiate seniors ego. Hence, keep fine tuning yourself as per environmental laws to move up the ladder. Redressal system is in place to ensure that if you get into the vicious circle, it will benefit the system more because everyone will try to make most of it by knowing and fully understanding your precarious situation and will exploit it.

A Costly Price for Sticking Out One's Neck

Both the Poonch and Anantnag reports were earned in an operational area going beyond the call of duty. It hurt me too much when I was communicated that the Anantnag report was endorsed as inflated. My CO wrote back strongly to MS Branch stating the reason why it should not be endorsed as inflated because it was earned in a most challenging situation.

The ACR reflects bravery of an exemplary order. It also finds a rare mention of leadership quality. Up the chain everyone was informed about eight months in advance viz mandatory 3 months regarding the officer being rated "OUTSTANDING". On many occasions, I was evaluated for confirmation and it was then that I earned an outstanding operational report. True to MS Branch reputation, the ACR was enfaced as 'Inflated! My CO wrote a detailed letter justifying the endorsement but no one has the time to reply why it was endorsed as inflated.

Before attaining next rank, one's performance in the previous command report is taken into cognizance. It's not these two command reports but also the next three staff appointment reports making it five in continuation were "OUTSTANDING". These reports became all the more significant when earned under different IO, RO and SROs and probably each one of them rated me "OUTSTANDING" still I failed to make to the rank of Colonel.

Alas! Still I did not make it to the next rank. I was outspoken and was always daring to face consequences. In about five years of service, I moved the court seeking justice. May be this move was not palatable to senior officers in the Army. Consequently, I was overlooked for the next rank as they felt promoting me would be at their peril. At least I draw solace from the fact that I got superseded because I stuck my neck out and dared to call 'spade a spade'.

The services require three distinct levels of leadership. The first is the level of execution, which is confined to the unit command level. This is really a functional level where Platoon, Company and Unit Commanders are in close touch with men and equipment, and it is on their performance in a battle that the fate of an operational plan depends. This level calls for a sound professional knowledge of weapons and skill in handling them, use of tactical ground and battle drills.

On the leadership side, a personal style which motivates a group to follow their Commander in the face of death is required. Over here, precept and example in facing the stresses and strains of crises, especially in physical courage and manpower management, assume great importance. At this level it is more essential to obey implicitly than to think for oneself but not to loose sight of welfare of troops. I strongly feel I did justice to my role as a Company Commander.

Not a 'Yes Man' but a *Panga* Taker!

Never a "yes sir" man, I was known for my no-nonsense attitude. In November 2002, I had refused to the then Corps Cdr in an open forum that my unit will not hold *Iftar* parties for locals in JandK. I was firmly against any *sadbhavna* or WHAMP activities. The Army was inducted into the Valley with an objective. In a bid to outdo each other, Army units started venturing into unsoldierly activities like providing education, canteen facilities, etc to locals. Understandably there might have been a need for these activities, but not purely for scoring brownie points. In my opinion this role should have been left for the local administration.

During my posting to Ladakh in 2009, to my horror, I found that the scope of *sadbhavna* had assumed dangerous proportions. Need of the hour was for military preparedness against two neighbouring countries and not to indulge in frivolous activities, like creating artificial glacier, etc. Shortage of officers needs to be explained against this backdrop. One as SO AWWA and one for "Op *Sadbhavna*"! Officers engagement in sedentary duties needs a relook. Even, the rates at which purchase of stores in the name of "Op *Sadbhavna* " were made needed to be scrutinised.

The term 'Panga Taker' is loosely used to refer to an officer who is known for indiscipline. Often I have borne this stigma, much to my dislike and discomfort. At no stage in my life I wanted to put self and my family at any disadvantage. Taking *panga* takes a lot from you - it is indeed energy sapping and more so in the Army life scenario, the difficulties increase manifold. Reason:

- You will not be granted leave when required for emergent purposes. Unlike other organisations, you cannot proceed w/o leave certificate.
- No administrative help will be extended. Since cantonments are cut off from the rest of city and any movement in and out demands security check, hence your day-to-day survival becomes difficult.

- You will be posted out to the place which no one wants to opt for. Even continuance in the same location is always under constant threat because under 'organisational interest' you can be posted out anytime.
- You will be assigned inconsequential tasks not befitting your rank and age. Whom to question?
- You are socially boycotted. No one would like to risk their career by being seen around with you. Here the family suffers the most.
- Fear of being subjected to false implication in any case remains high. The whole army machinery is at seniors disposal.
- Swallow pride because you stand to lose as you are guaranteed to get no 'eye witness' support nor any documentary evidence.

The list is endless!

You live only once. Live right! At the end of the day, everyone is laid to rest. Hence, make life meaningful. Don't do anything wrong but think twice before accepting anything wrong remained my fundamental principle of life.

The Past is Over and Done With

Most of the time it is not true. Life comes a full circle. When I moved the Allahabad High Court, I thought this will put an end to everything but that was not to be. I moved to another unit but the past still haunted me because my complaint was processed through my present unit.

After staff course, I tried hard to focus on my professional career and wrote to this effect to MS Branch (Refer page 122), but true to their reputation they remained oblivious to my genuine request. My premature moving out of HQ 2 Sect RR could have been avoided.

In view of no redressal in spite of the continued stand against fraudulent purchases made, I started preparing for the civvie street without realising that once again

I will take up the cause via this medium of writing a book.

The past is never over and done with.

You have to live with it!

I have lived my service career to full contentment, although unfortunately a career of a superseded officer.

1988	–	Volunteered to do jumps from parachute.
1990	–	Successfully underwent commando training.
1994	–	Moved the Allahabad High Court against Col VK Singh for his wife's misconduct.
1994	–	At Siachen Glacier volunteered to be Commander at an operational location from where two officers got evacuated. Re-sited one location amidst enemy firing where even Cdr failed to reach.
1998	–	Incharge of Rock Climbing School till Kargil War.
1999	–	Brought out irregularities in mountaineering equipment purchases.
2000	–	Killed terrorists.
2001	–	Qualified for prestigious DSSC.
2002	–	Killed a renowned terrorist.
2004	–	Prematurely moved out on my own on account of Commander's misdemeanour.
2006	–	Refused to be party to the incorrect usage of training fund.
2008	–	Volunteered to serve in high altitude area.
2011	–	Addressed the people during Anna Hazare's fasting at Ramlila Maidan on 23 August, 2011.

I look back with complete sense of achievement.

CHAPTER 3

Matter of Honour

A soldier lays down his life smilingly and considers it to be an honourable death. If a soldier is tuned to face the only certainty of life, that is death, in such a befitting manner he is accordingly expected to put a brave front to the challenges of life.

In this chapter, I will narrate what compelled me always to take challenges head on. First, let us talk about Army Chief Gen VK Singh, who had created much hype regarding his age until the Supreme Court advised him to withdraw his petition as the available evidence was against his stand in the date of birth row.

Gen VK Singh is professionally very competent. His professional knowledge and caliber puts him above the rest. As a CO he used to outshine his peers during conduct of operational briefings. A lot to learn from him on professional front. But, he was altogether a different man when he moved to a peace station. His wife's influence over him leaves his personal conduct under scrutiny! A fact which is well known in Army.

Not So Rosy Past of Gen VK Singh

Senior officers were against posting Lt Col VK Singh, YSM, to 2 Rajput as CO since it was he who had damaged the reputation of the battalion due to his stubbornness and arrogance. The Col of the Regt was of the opinion that Lt Col VK Singh would not be acceptable as CO to the jawans of 2 Rajput. He was reluctant to post him as CO. But thanks to his clout, Lt Col VK Singh made it to 2 Rajput as CO overcoming all odds. The posting was much to the dislike of the jawans as well as the officers of the battalion. Col Thomas Mathew convinced everyone in the battalion that Col VK Singh was a changed man and had promised to take people along. Col Thomas Mathew also took over the battalion amidst controversy but his performance on the personal front remained satisfactory.

High Headed: Col VK Singh was out and out high-headed. He felt that nobody is worth anything except him. The battalion started faring badly in all professional and sports competitions. Being his Staff Officer, I was appalled to see his conduct as a CO.

Insecure: Never ever Col VK Singh stayed at any Company HQ post – either he was scared that troops disliked him because of Maj D P Kukrety case (mentioned later in the chapter) or he felt insecure. He remained aloof, hardly interacting with the troops, resulting in a mysterious death case in the battalion. The case concerned the death of an INT Jawan in mysterious circumstances.

Manipulative: Here are some facts that prove the manipulative calibre of Col VK Singh:

- Since the INT Jawan case did not go down well with the seniors, Col VK Singh evaded earning an ACR in 1991.
- Even when his posting order was issued as CO-24 Rajput, he approached VCOAS and got the posting order cancelled.
- Throughout his career he got posted under a Commander of his choice. As CO and Bde Cdr he served under Lt Gen DS Chauhan.
- His regimental duties were far too less and he mostly managed postings at family stations.
- Interestingly, he managed to get his own ACR overlooked which was written after he was duly warned of his failure on the professional front. (In his presence, the troops of 2 Rajput and 7 Kumaon got into fist-fight during a boxing match).

Banyan Tree: Col VK Singh was likened to be a banyan tree under which nothing grows. Hardly any Company Commander under him made it to the next rank, i.e. Lt Col, nor any of his two seconds-in-command got the next rank. Even his SM and HC did not get honorary rank. No officer made it to DSSC during his tenure.

Worst Command Tenure

The battalion command is the last command wherein you are directly in touch with the troops. The battalion command tenure is considered an acid test in one's Army career. Trust is a priceless personal quality that is attributed to one by one's colleagues. Col VK Singh never enjoyed the trust of his subordinates resultant of which his battalion command was marred by many ugly incidents. For a leader the biggest satisfaction and contentment stems from the fact that he is widely accepted and followed by the men he commands. One looks back at this tenure with pride and satisfaction and always boasts about it. Sadly, Col VK Singh's Command was the worst one can think of. Central Army Commander Lt Gen YN Sharma, during his visit to the battalion, termed in no uncertain terms Col VK Singh's Command a failure and threatened to disband the battalion after the boxing incident with 7 Kumaon.

As stated earlier, the battalion, in gross violation of discipline, was involved in a hand-to-hand fight with another battalion in a boxing match. 2 Coy Cdrs and SM of the Bn was attached. But thanks to his manipulative acumen, Col VK Singh made it to higher command course despite his all-round failure as the battalion Commander.

A mysterious death in the battalion; the battalion sending no officer to DSSC; and SM and Coy Cdrs getting attached to another formation/unit, but the CO, Col VK Singh making it to higher command! Isn't it being tactful and manipulative?

Enough is Enough

Now I turn to another role of Col VK Singh. I had performed well in the courses and was the only officer who had won the division level MMG competition in April 1992. Due to my resourcefulness and professional maturity, I was considered indispensable by Col VK Singh. He sent me as part of the advance party to facilitate the unit move from Jammu to Faizabad. However, after having successfully completed my assigned task, I was asked to move back and settle certain murky issues of the unit as part of the rear team. Even though I was rated low in figurative assessment by Col VK Singh in January 1992, I continued to perform well and was assigned important tasks in Feb 1992. But, when he chose to step out of the line unethically, under his wife's influence, I came out by writing the following demi-official (DO) letter to him:

CONFIDENTIAL

CAPT. ARUN KUMAR 2 RAJPUT
C/O 56 APO

48368 / PRS / 40 / 03 16 Jan 1994

Dear Sir,

1. At the outset I tender my apology in having taken the liberty of bothering your kind-self like this, but the existing circumstances have left me with no other option except to resort to this communication.

2. I am serving under you from July 1991, but from the period commencing from July 1993, I have been subjected to various types of indignities which may be found serialised as under:

   a) After my part of annual leave in third week of July 1993, I had observed that while I was on leave (w.e.f. 13 June to 8 July) the unit generator has been taken to your residence and diesel was also taken from the unit MT, which was commented upon by me which infuriated your kind-self[1]. I now infer that it was your annoyance as a result of which I was removed from the responsibilities of MTO and posted to "C" coy as a coy officer just within a week and a DO Part I to this effect was later published vide BRO 155/93 dated 7 August 1993. It is submitted that I had carried out the duties of MTO successfully w.e.f. September 1992 and even performed this function when battalion took over the present location from 1 MARATHA LI. I wish to mention here that my abrupt removal from MT was executed fully knowing that CEME

1 **Moral Courage.** I had the moral courage as a young officer with five years of service to bring impropriety to the notice of my Commanding Officer Col VK Singh. But he could not gather courage as a Lt Gen to put across his point of view on the date of birth issue. He only made a mockery of himself by saying that he gave the undertaking regarding his date of birth under duress.

inspection was on 5 August 1993 and only JCOs were left to look after unit MT. Later, my presence being inescapable necessity I was reinstated for the duration of inspection (CEME).

b) I regret that your annoyance had percolated to the extent that even my wife was humiliated on 20 July during the unit ladies get-together at the Officers Mess by your wife, Mrs VK Singh, where she told my wife to leave the Officers' Mess. Again on 26 July during Major SS Sandhu's daughter's birthday party at their residence when all the unit officers/families and children were present, Mrs VK Singh insulted me and my wife when you had left the place and gone inside Major Sandhu's study room[2].

c) On 17 June 1993 during Inter-battalion Boxing finals between 7 Kumaon and 2 Rajput, a situation had arisen, which necessitated visit of GOC 1 Corps on 14 August 1993. On 15 August 1993 you had taken an interview with the GOC in Dogra Regimental Centre VIP guest room, followed by interview of GOC 1 Corps with CO7 Kumaon and 2IC 7 Kumaon. After your interview you had called me (I was performing the duties of LO to Mrs Veena Sandhu, wife of GOC 1 Corps) and desired to me to go behind in the kitchen[3] and hear the conversation between the GOC and CO and 2I/c 7 Kumaon. I at once expressed my inability, as such action would have been unbecoming of an officer. This refusal from me further infuriated you, because you had retorted that "friend, watch out now".

d) Thereafter, the humiliation gained momentum. We were boycotted socially. Unit officers were instructed

2 **Man of the House.** As CO, Col VK Singh's house bore the name plates of 'RAJPUT HOUSE' and Col VK SINGH. You were head of the family of the unit. But as a responsible head of the family you were not supposed to leave your own helpless officers and their wives at the mercy of your wife and go inside hiding in study room. Come on! You are man of the house. Don't let your officers be easy prey to your wife (alter ego).

3 **Unbecoming of an Officer.** As I stated at page 104, basic traits of a human being never change. Gen VK Singh at the Indian Military Academy was considered to be tactful. This was quite evident from his writ petition filed in the Supreme Court on the date of birth issue in which he sought all consequential benefits, considering his year of birth as 1951.

not to visit us. I sustained the humiliation but it was intolerable for my wife and this led to severe depression and she was evacuated to the Military Hospital and admitted on 11 September 1993. My wife's condition had no effect on you which is apparent from the fact that you declined to grant me part of annual leave which was an inescapable requirement to look after my wife. On my repeated requests for leave, you had retorted that her ailment and admission in the Military Hospital was nothing else but a drama. Instead, I was out on ITC Camp from 18 Sept 1993 to 2 Oct 1993.

e) Similarly, my brother-in-law was engaged on 24 Oct for which my wife had to go alone and attend it as you refused me 4 days casual leave.

f) I may record here that you were in Delhi during your leave w.e.f. 20 Oct 1993 to 29 Oct 1993 in view of cancellation of your posting and it was on 27 Oct 1993 that my posting order for 23 Rajput was issued vide AHQ letter No. 32549/23 Rajput/MS 2C dt. 27 Oct 1993 copy[4] of which was neither received in the battalion nor in the Bde HQs (apparently not even in the Div. HQ and CENTRAL COMMAND). Obviously the intention being to take me by surprise. Moreover:

   (i) The above posting could not be manipulated unless some "false information" was furnished because only volunteers are posted to "Siachen" as such it appears that "someone" having vested interest must have furnished "false information".

   (ii) The copy of posting order, dated 27 Oct 1993, was not received in the unit till 14 December 1993, wherein copy of the same had reached 23 Rajput in the first week of November 1993, which creates reasonable doubts about the manipulation of this posting.

---

4 **Manipulative.** Col VK Singh got his own posting to JC Wing cancelled by literally requesting the next in line incumbent to give an undertaking for delay in taking over by nine months. And, on the other hand, he ensured that my posting order never reaches the unit so as to take me by surprise and thereby giving me no reaction time to represent against his malafide intention.

(iii) It is also understood that even a demi-official letter written from CO 23 Rajput "apparently welcoming me" never reached my hands but your having sent signal No. A-0121 dt. 28 Nov. 1993 asking for a copy of my posting order from 23 Rajput, info MS Branch conclusively establishes malafide and questionable motives, especially when I had after serving for 4 years and 3 months in hard peace/field area /OP RAKSHAK) had come to this location on 18 Feb 1993.

(iv) Your issuing of the movement order to me on 27 Dec 1993 (I was on leave till 26 Dec 1993 and on 27 Dec I had requested you for 7 days furlough leave vide my letter 48368/PRS/28/03 dt. 27 Dec. 1993 to bring my family back to the station) and declaring me S.O.S. w.e.f. 27 Dec (AN) itself vividly establishes the motive behind, ironically when the date of reporting was 15 Jan 1994.

(v) Contrary to rules[5], movement order was issued earlier and clearance sought later by 1000 h on 28 Dec. 1993.

g) My appearing in promotion examination Part D was attempted to be jeopardised by you as after my application form duly filled/countersigned by you for Allahabad on 07 Dec 1993, the centre being Allahabad being notified by HQ 4 Arty Bde vide their letter No. 104720/gs (ops) dt. 16 Dec 1993.

(i) Firstly, by attempting me to move out by handing me movement order for 23 Rajput on 27 Dec (AN).

(ii) Secondly, sending a signal to 3 Inf. Div for change of centre without my willingness although there was a provision to take up case

5 **Rules are Rules.** Col VK Singh gave a damn to all the rules in the book by pushing me out prematurely and went to the extent of not even honouring MS Branch letter. However, in the age row, he wanted the country to believe all his lame excuses regarding his claim over his DOB.

with MS Branch for deferment of posting in view of examination.

(iii) It may be noted the movement order was handed in advance and the confirmation of my change of centre came later on 29 Dec/30 Dec 1993. (Signal No. 0-4011)

(iv) At no stage I had filled a fresh form for change of my centre (Ref. SAO 2/5/85).

(v) Thirdly, by refusing to accept AHQ signal no. 381452/MS 2C dt 4 Jan 1994 from me at 1330h on 05 Jan 1994. Perforce the same was handed over to the Bde Duty clerk on 5 Jan 1994 at 1500 h.

(vi) Even after my posting was held you had attempted to send me to Leh for appearing in Part D examination by way of handing over a movement order dated 7 Jan at 1115 h, making it impossible for me to reach Leh. Had I to appear from Leh, I would have been issued the movement order either on 5 Jan (AN) or 6 Jan (FN).

(vii) My request for allowing me to appear from Allahabad was turned down (my letter No. 48368/PRS/37/03 dt. 7 Jan 1994) and was finally granted 6 days casual leave as late as 1530h on 9 Jan 1994, which is against the existing regulations as I was entitled to a movement order. Wherein on the other hand I had to appear at my own expenses.

h) Even after the directions of AHQ sig no. 381452 / MS 2C dt. 4 Jan 1994 holding my "manipulated posting" to Siachen Glacier, you had not allowed me to join the battalion. The Adjt was instructed by you and again on 6 Jan 1994 when I reported I was told to go. Finally, on 7 Jan 1994 I was taken on strength.

3. In view of my submission in the preceding paragraphs I reasonably apprehend that personal vendetta is bound to overtake your logic reasoning and may be even humane

approach, which may result into subjective "Annual Confidential Report", as such I earnestly request that in the larger interest of justice and fair play it may not be initiated by you.

Sd/...

Col VK Singh, YSM
CO
2 RAJPUT
C/O 56 APO

CONFIDENTIAL

Allahabad High Court Aspersion: The Allahabad High Court, while considering my petition against the Siachen posting, went on record to state that the above mentioned confidential letter casts aspersions on Col VK Singh's personal and professional integrity. (The HC judgement is reproduced at page 71)

My Subjective ACR by the Col Set Aside

Owing to the nature of work, subjectivity in ACR is bound to exist. Unlike the civvie street where appraisal is target-oriented, in the Army in some cases it depends on the whims of the IO. My ACR of the year 1994, initiated by Col VK Singh, is a solid proof of this officer-centred subjectivity. I had an inkling of this subjectivity creeping into my 1994 ACR. That's why I had written the above DO letter in an attempt to restrain Col VK Singh from initiating my ACR. However, ignoring my letter, he went on to write my ACR.

I had won the MMG competition at the Division level and was appreciated via Pt 1 order by Col V K Singh. Later on, differences cropped up between us due to a non-military issue. As stated in the above DO letter, I had taken a tough stand against the misconduct of Col VK Singh's wife who had insultingly asked my wife to leave the Officer's Mess as she reached late for a get-together. My ACR was a stark reflection of this non-military issue. Nowhere in the ACR, my professional credentials got a mention. Instead, I was reported upon about my impropriety. An officer with 5 years of service was probably not aware of this linguistic jugglery! But the ACR was rightly set aside as being subjective. However, was Col VK Singh asked for his impropriety in writing this highly subjective ACR?

Col Singh's Remarkable Immunity to Adverse ACRs

Interestingly, the same year (1994), Col VK Singh also earned an adverse ACR wherein he was given low figurative assessment after having been warned in writing for his failure of command. In true sense, it was Col VK Singh's failure of command. Going by the Army discipline, soldiers in front of their CO don't dare blink. But in the case of CO, Col VK Singh, his soldiers in his very presence locked horns with the soldiers of another unit (the boxing match incident). As a CO he should have been removed from Command for failing to command troops. But, despite an ACR on command failure, he got nominated for higher command, making a mockery of the whole Army system.

On expected lines, Col VK Singh got the ACR expunged. He is the first Army Chief who has got expunged not one but few ACRs to attain the top most rank. He has filed many non-statutory complaints in life as he is fully aware of the lacunae in the system and exploits them to his advantage all the time. The same Indian Army which had bailed him out many a time was subjected to humiliation by him over the date of birth issue.

In the same reporting year (1994), another officer, Capt Anurag Chauhan of my service bracket, was sent on two courses of instruction in spite of his "C" grading in the previous course of instruction. He was sent on the second course in the same year to help him avoid earning an ACR (reviewed by the RO who had come to know about the true Colours of Col VK Singh and his stooges).

With total disregard to rules, this officer was graded "outstanding" next year by making his ACR due as Major. The officer was RTU from the second course on medical grounds. It was a manipulation blatantly carried out. Had he not been sent on the second course of instruction he would have had to earn an ACR from the Bde Cdr. In all likelihood, he would have been rated very low as he was the one who instigated the fight between the troops of 2 Rajput and 7 Kumaon. Summary of evidence was recorded for this against this officer. Col VK Singh later rated this very officer 'Outstanding'. On physical fitness front Capt Anurag Chauhan was unable to pass a single test when tested upon during Annual Inspection. Ironically, the same reporting year I got the Bn MMG team the first position in the entire Infantry Division but I had to face Col VK Singh's wrath as he failed to keep his family life separate from his professional life.

To be in the CO's good book, Serve "Super CO"

The "super CO" referred to in the above heading is no one else but the CO's better half, that is, his wife. As is clear from my DO letter presented above, I have paid heavily for my inability to serve my "super CO". As young soldiers, we grow up knowing the traditions and rich culture of the Army in general and our battalion in particular. Espirit de corps is what we live and die for. Against this backdrop, the institution of CO is the most sacred place and the officer holding it is considered to be a "demi god". But the esteem of this office takes a beating when the better half of the CO assumes the role of "super CO" either due to her implanted ego or improper upbringing. At times she goes berserk having no regard for the battalion's reputation and makes the battalion an object of ridicule.

In uniform you don't mind going beyond the call of duty even on a non-professional issue on the orders of your CO. At times you kill your conscience and even toe the line of the CO's wife. But it's not same with your better half who may find it uncouth to go along the whims and fancies of the "super CO". You have no answer to your wife's poser, "How can she ("super CO") expect anyone's wife to be subservient to her?"

Obviously, an officer is duty-bound to respect his CO and follow his commands. But it is when the CO's wife mistakenly expects the same behaviour from the officer's wife, fissures develop. Now if you don't have an understanding CO or even if he understands but is highly influenced by his wife's overbearing attitude then you are in for trouble. An RTI will reveal how many non-stats/stats are of this nature. In my case Col VK Singh remained dumb-founded when Mrs VK Singh took over the command after office hours.

AWWA influence: It is due to the patronage provided by the Army Wives Welfare Association (AWWA) that sometimes wives of senior officers become arrogant and misuse their influence. The AWWA has become a parallel chain of command in the Army, and senior officers' wives have been asserting their influence on the administration. It is not good for the Army.

The AWWA is nothing else but an organization carved out to assuage the egos of these Army ladies. They represent the Colonial legacy. The unwritten saying is that an Army officer's wife holds one rank higher than her husband. This saying is reflected in the tantrums displayed by her courtesy AWWA. This organisation is a menace whose functioning needs to be monitored.

Going Back on Promise

I continued to perform my duties but when I received my posting order again in March 1994, I realised that all this while Col VK Singh was trying to fulfil his single-point agenda, that is, to post me out. Though on the surface, after my posting was held in abeyance, he promised me that he would put the lid on the whole issue and asked me to move on with a clean slate. Though unit officers and their wives had warned me to be careful, I took Col VK Singh's word for granted, not realising that he had never kept his word. Soon he came in his true colour when he wrote to COAS to intervene to ensure my posting to Siachen despite promising me the opposite.

Imagine! On my complaint to MS Branch that my posting was a consequence of his wife's misbehaviour with my wife, his reply was sent to all addresses up the chain by NOO. Therefore he misled and hoodwinked everyone. The reason of sending the reply up the chain on NOO was to apprise the higher headquarters about his biased point of view to cover up the actual issue of his wife's high-headedness because everybody in the Faizabad Cantt knew about his wife's arrogant behaviour. His primary aim was to influence Div Headquarters, Corps HQ and Command HQ about his concocted version so as to succeed in posting me out. This letter/ reply was sent by his 2 IC, Lt Col AK Singh. Here too he shied away from his duty.

Col VK Singh even went to the extent of placing guards outside my house and his stooges started sending threats to me. I immediately filed a non-stat complaint which he cleverly sent to HQ 114 Inf Bde so that his superiors do not come to know about his true colour. (That complaint is yet to be traced back - what an irony!) I attached my DO dated 16 January 1994 clearly stating his misuse of government property in this non-stat complaint.

Moved the Allahabad High Court

Col VK Singh's uncalled for actions compelled and forced me to knock the doors of the Allahabad High Court mainly with a premise to make people aware of what he is made up of. Thankfully, God was kind and in an expeditious manner the verdict was out.

A Captain taking his CO to the court for justice is unthinkable and unheard of. Herein the reason becomes more important as the issue behind pushing me out of the battalion was purely due to Col VK Singh's wife's misbehaviour with my wife. That is why I have stated in my book that a parallel hierarchy with respect to ladies should not exist in Army.

HC Judgement

The Allahabad High Court judgement is as follows:

The petitioner, at present a Captain in the 2 Battalion, Rajput regiment of the Indian Army, was commissioned in the Indian Army on the 17th December, 1988 and on the same day posted to the battalion of the aforesaid regiment. According to the petitioner he served with the battalion in extreme climatic conditions in the Jammu and Kashmir area for four years and six months. In November 1992, the petitioner was sent as advance party Commander to a peace station in Uttar Pradesh, under command and control of the 4 Infantry Division, and after making detailed arrangements for moving of the main body of the 2 Battalion of the Rajput Regiment returned to Jammu and Kashmir region. This was followed by the 2 Battalion of the Rajput Regiment moving from Jammu and Kashmir area to peace area station tenure in UP, the petitioner going with his battalion. The petitioner states that on reaching the peace station location all went well with him and his battalion. In fact, the petitioner has pointed out that the petitioner in a sense distinguished himself by leading the team which won the first position in the 4 Infantry Division inter-battalion firing competition as evidenced by an order/congratulatory message dated 17th April, 1993, inter alia, recording the above fact and congratulating the winning team, a copy of which order is found as Annexure 1 to the writ petition.

The petition then goes on to recite that during the middle of the year 1993, the petitioner noticed that the actions of Col VK Singh (respondent no. 5) and others regarding, what he calls "misuse of government property", and expressed his concern over such misuse, which according to the petitioner, was frowned upon by respondent no. 5. Indeed, the petition goes on to recite that because of the aforementioned respondent no. 5 was greatly annoyed and wanted "to teach the petitioner a lesson." Some of the instances of harassment, ill-treatment and humiliation[6] meted out to the petitioner by CO VK Singh, the 5th respondent herein, find mention in the petitioner's letter written to the 5th respondent, which letter was marked "Confidential" a copy of which letter is annexed as Annexure 3 to this petition. The letter also briefly indicated the background against which the various events transpired. Thus, the letter mentions two or three things which annoyed Col VK Singh and disposed him to take a vengeful attitude against the petitioner. For instance the letter mentions:

a) After my part of annual leave in the third week of July 1993, I had observed that while I was on leave (w.e.f. 13th June to 08th July 1993) the unit generator has been taken to your residence and diesel was also taken from the unit MT, which was commented upon by me which infuriated your kind self. I now infer that it was your annoyance as a result of which, I was removed from the responsibilities of MTO and posted to "C" coy as a coy officer just within a week and a DO Part I to this effect was later published vide BRO 155/93 dated 07th August 1993. It is submitted that I had carried out the duties to MTO successfully w.e.f. September 1992 and even performed this function when battalion took over the present location from 1 MARATHA LI. I wish to mention here that my abrupt removal from MT was executed fully knowing the CEME inspection was on 05th August 1993

6 **Ill-treatment of Subordinates.** Blatant misuse of office to ensure that I and my wife were subjected to continuous harassment. As a result of this, my wife had to be admitted to Military hospital for depression.

and only JCOs were left to look after the MT. Later, my presence being inescapable necessity I was reinstated for the duration of inspection (CEME).

b) I regret that your annoyance had percolated to the extent that even my wife was humiliated on 20 July during the unit ladies get-together at the Officers Mess by your wife, Mrs VK Singh, where she told my wife to leave the Officers Mess. Again on 26 July during Major SS Sandhu's daughter's birthday party at their residence when all the unit officers/families and children were present, Mrs VK Singh insulted me and my wife when you had left the place and gone inside Major Sandhu's study room.

The said letter proceeds after giving some further incidents constituting the background of the 5th respondent's annoyance with the petitioner to record the 5th respondent's retort "Friend, watch out now", and goes on the record that humiliation heaped upon the petitioner thereafter gained momentum and the petitioner and his wife were boycotted socially and unit officers were instructed not to visit them. The petitioner, according to him, sustained the humiliation but it became intolerable for his wife and this led to severe depression and she had to be admitted to the Military Hospital on 11th September, 1993. The letter in page after page (every one of them marked "Confidential") goes on to record several other instances of harassment to the petitioner and goes on to conclude with the words:

> "In view of my submission in the preceding paragraphs, I reasonably apprehend that personal vendetta is bound to overtake your logic (and) reasoning and maybe even humane approach, which may result into subjective "Annual Confidential Report", as such I earnestly request that in the larger interest of justice and fair play it may not be initiated by you."

The petition goes on to complain that not satisfied with heaping harassment, humiliation and ill-treatment upon the petitioner, respondent no. 5 manipulated the posting of the petitioner to Siachen Glacier which would have been done as per the policy in existence only if the petitioner had volunteered for the same and in point of fact the petitioner had never volunteered for such posting. The petitioner has averred in paragraph 8 of the petition that opposite party no. 5 furnished false information[7] to the Army Headquarters that the petitioner was a volunteer, based upon which information the posting order was issued. To spell out a case of the existence of the policy not to post any member of the armed forces in the glacier region unless he had volunteered, the petitioner has, inter alia, placed reliance upon a letter written to him by Maj Gen RS Taragi and has also invoked Article 14 of the Constitution of India on the question of the enforcement of the policy though he has not given any specific instances in support of his argument of Article 14 of the Constitution of India to indicate that the petitioner has been discriminated against. From the prayers, quoted at the commencement of this judgement, one notices that the petitioner has sought the issue of a mandamus mixing the same with the violation of the policy of the respondents with regard to not posting out officers who have not volunteered. When a writ of mandamus is sought, the question that normally arises for consideration is whether the respondents in their public character and office are under a statutory duty to act or to desist from acting in a particular manner; and when one considers questions of policy coupled with an argument under Article 14 of the Constitution of India, one is reminded of the fact the existence of all policy by itself does not always confer a statutorily enforceable right; and when considering an argument under Article 14 of the Constitution of India, one looks for specific instance/s indicating that the

7 **False Information.** Gen VK Singh while filling his IMA Dossier had in his own handwriting filled up 1950 as DOB. He gave a lame excuse that this was filled up because it had to be in consonance with the date mentioned in the UPSC form which was filled up by his teacher as 1950. When did he come to know that his teacher has filled up 1950 as his DOB?

petitioner has been discriminated against in the light of the treatment meted out to other persons similarly situate and that there is no nexus or connection between the policy of law and the discrimination so made. We must, however, hasten to add that, in our view, postings in the Indian Army may not always appropriately be the subject of either the issue of a writ of mandamus or an inquiry in the nature involved in an action for the issue of writ of certiorari. It is our considered view that the special powers reserved under Article 226 of the Constitution of India to writ courts should not routinely be invoked for interference in the matter of posting in the Indian Army and the writ court must exercise its discretionary powers most sparingly and only in exceptional cases, where matters of posting are concerned. The Indian Army has a proud and glorious tradition[8] dating right back through the corridors of time and particularly in the matter of posting, the time honoured adage reminds one that whereas it is the privilege of a few to command, it is the duty of those commanded to submit and obey; that being the fibre of which discipline[9] is made. Army discipline and spirit generally have been immortalised in the "Charge of the Light Bridge" which begins with the words "Half a league, half a league, half a league onward, "Into the Valley of Death rode the six hundred..." To serve in the Indian Army is a privilege given to but a few and to be posted in difficult and dangerous terrain may itself be considered as a preferment conferring distinction in itself. These are not matters where we would feel inclined to interfere except in the most compelling circumstances and it is our considered view that army postings should not lightly be interfered with in the exercise of writ jurisdiction. What is more, in the instant case we cannot

8 The Indian Army is well known for its **ethos and rich traditions**. But Gen VK Singh's actions concerning the age issue have put a big question mark regarding the credibility of the Indian Army. However, during the same time Solicitor General **Gopal Subramaniam** resigned as he felt the dignity of his office was being compromised and undermined.

9 Once again Gen VK Singh has **faltered** on this account.

lose sight of the fact that the petitioner's application went up for consideration right up to the Army Headquarters which for a period of a time even issued orders of stay and the petitioner's matter received the personal attention of no less a person than the Chief of Army Staff (who has been made party, respondent no. 2) in the person of Gen BC Joshi, PVSM, AVSM, known to be a first class human being and General par excellence. In the light of the above observations, we do not consider it appropriate to interfere in the exercise of writ jurisdiction in the matter of the posting of the petitioner, the petitioner having proceeded to the posting at the Siachen Glacier in early March, 1994. Having said this, we think it appropriate to notice a few things indicated herein below.

As stated earlier, the petitioner's case is based upon the existence of a policy[10] which makes posting in the glacier region dependent upon volunteering on the part of the individual intended to be posted out and of the petitioner having been short-listed for the purpose out of considerations definitely lacking in bona fides in spite of the fact that the petitioner had not volunteered for such posting. For spelling out the existence of the policy aforesaid, the petitioner, apart from quoting from the letter from Maj Gen Taragi, which in its early portion states "I agree with you that in spite of your being a non-volunteer you have been posted to 23 Rajput for their glacier tenure..." has also sought to quote chapter and verse on the matter of spelling out the precise provisions constituting the policy in this behalf. For our purpose, we do not find it necessary to go into details regarding this policy, for we wish to concern ourselves with the reply put forward substantially by his respondent no. 5 or on his behalf. The learned counsel for the respondents has

10 **Existence of Policy.**
Then Col VK Singh could not convince the Allahabad High Court about my volunteering to Siachen Glacier.
Now Gen VK Singh once again tried but failed to convince the nation by deviating from the existing policy and going back on his commitment made to the government.

placed before us for our perusal the file of papers relating to Capt Arun Kumar's posting and although it was not specifically referred to and relied on in the affidavit filed on behalf of the respondents, in the interests of justice we have looked into the same at the behest of the learned counsel for the respondents. With regard to the posting of officers the first document in the said file when recording at point no. 5 of the document about "Discussion about posting to 23 RAJPUT" states that "the CO informed the officers about the letter he received from the Colonel of the regiment asking for suitable officers for a tenure with 23 Rajput. CO informed all present that in keeping with our tradition there should be no qualms in being a volunteer in our unit and we had earlier sent two officers for this. He asked the officers if anyone had any objection[11] to this or wants to say anything. No officer present raised any objections." Reliance is placed on the above excerpt in support of the submission that the petitioner had volunteered. One cannot help noticing that the volunteering consisted of the exhortation of the CO (respondent no. 5 herein) underlining that in keeping with the tradition there should be no qualms in being volunteer and asking if any officer had any objection and no officer present raising any objection. As against this, let us see what Col VK Singh writes in his letter addressed to Gen BC Joshi, PVSM/AVSM, Chief of the Army Staff Army Headquarters, DBO PO New Delhi, which letter commences with the words, "My dear Chief, (this being the letter dated the 7th of January, 1994). The first paragraph of this letter commences with the statement that Col VK Singh feels constrained to write directly to the Chief of Army Staff since the issue pertains to the latter's concern for upholding the institution of the Commanding Officer as

11 **Concocted Story**

Then Col VK Singh gave an unconvincing and unreliable story regarding my volunteering to Siachen Glacier in spite of the Col of the Regiment clearly stating the contrary.

Now Gen VK Singh in the age row was hellbent to put across his view-point by giving all sorts of stories by stating that he was compelled to give an undertaking for accepting his year of birth as 1950.

well as to restore the faith in the credibility of Army system[12] of postings. In the next paragraph he refers to his case that the officer of his unit Capt Arun Kumar volunteered to go to 23 Rajput, along with other young officers." The letter goes on to recite, "... based on my Colonel of Regiments giving priority..." (one can hardly fail to notice that "Volunteering" which consisted of no officer raising any objection has now been converted into officers expressing "great keenness" and "accordingly" a few names being.... forwarded. In the same paragraph Col VK Singh goes on to suggest that the petitioner started running around to get his posting cancelled "under the influence of his wife." (The letter throws no light on what has prompted this assertion on the part of the fifth respondent.) Having set up a foundation and an atmosphere[13] in paragraph 2, excerpts whereof have been quoted above respondent no. 5 goes on to highlight in paragraph 4 (a) and (c) of the said letter as follows:

a) An officer can say something[14] in front of his Commanding Officer and then go around presenting false facts subsequently. It also sets a precedent for other officers to volunteer and then change their minds[15]. This will further erode the values sought to be revived.

c) This will even percolate to the men. They suffer greater hardships and they see officers giving false statement can get their way avoiding supposedly difficult posting, they will also do their bit in following suit.

---

12 The High Court clearly saw through Col VK Singh's gimmick in his letter written in my case to the then Chief of Army Staff Gen BC Joshi and termed it dramatic. Years later, his letter (now in public domain) to Gen Deepak Kapoor regarding age settlement was not an honest commitment as he never meant to follow it.

13 Col VK Singh possessed an uncanny knack of putting across things in a manner so to extract the most on an emotional note. In the present context, his letter to Gen Deepak Kapoor was nothing but setting up a foundation and an atmosphere to extract the most when the time comes.

14 **Word of Honour.** Relate this to Gen VK Singh's own commitment that he made to the then Army Chief Gen Deepak Kapoor about some misgivings and doubts being raised on his commitment given on date of birth.

15 Ironically, Gen VK Singh committed in writing and afterwards having changed his mind had gone to SC. Old habits die hard!

The letter ends on an emotional note[16] that the faith and honour reposed in the Commanding Officer will be upheld. For respondent no. 5 to affirm in the aforesaid letter that the officers expressed "great keenness" was less than fair to the petitioner and did not present a true and faithful picture of what had actually transpired.

Perhaps the Colonel got carried away by his keenness to ensure that the petitioner's posting was not changed, or perhaps he thought the above affirmation as necessary to lay the foundation from which to launch the two dramatic statements reproduced herein above from paragraph 4 (a) and (c). Be that as it may the fact remains that respondent no. 5 assertions about the officers having expressed great keenness is not borne out by the earlier quoted passage where the volunteering is said to consist of no officer present raising any objections. This conduct on the part of the 5th respondent is less than fair or honourable[17] and certainly does not measure up to the highest traditions of the Indian Army. Indeed, we feel a bit let down at noticing the above. We do believe that discipline on the part of the subordinate officers in the Army and fair play and justice on the part of the seniors are but two sides of the same coin and may be compared to the two wheels of the chariot of efficiency in the Army, the progress whereof is bound to be hampered if both do not function smoothly and in harmony or if even one of them is found to be malfunctioning[18]. We have been

---

16 **Emotional Note** The Allahabad High Court could quickly assess the transition from volunteering to great keenness and saw Col VK Singh's hidden malafide intention. Presently, the letter written to Gen Deepak Kapoor by him is on the similar lines, that is, on an emotional note, so as to make him believe of his commitment at that point of time.

17 **Honour and Dignity.** Col VK Singh himself did not file the counter affidavit and asked one of his subordinates to file it. My counsel pointed to the bench that why he had not filed the counter affidavit despite being present in the court. Look today who is talking of integrity and honour.

18 The situation arose because Col VK Singh went back on his word of not taking up the issue of my posting any further. Similarly, now after having given commitment in writing to COAS, he is going back on his commitment by appealing to SC — **Malfunctioning**!

prompted to make these observations because we feel that when we extend the fullest respect to the Indian Army and its traditions in refusing to interfere in the matter of posting except for compelling reasons, we feel entitled to expect nothing but honourable conduct, particularly from the higher echelons of the Indian Army. One wonders what the decision of Gen BC Joshi, PVSM, AVSM, would have been if Col VK Singh had instead of adding his flourishes confined himself to the facts as purported to have been recorded earlier where the "volunteering" on the part of the petitioner is stated to have consisted of his not objecting. When on the subject of "volunteering", it would not be out of place to mention that, to our mind, "volunteering" can only mean a person voluntarily offering his services or offering to enrol in anything (e.g. the Armed Forces) and a thing cannot be said to have been done "voluntarily" unless it is done by the person of his own free will and accord – it can only be "unintentional" (not constrained) or "purposed". In other words, it involves something being done by one's own volition. The concept of silence being consent can never be stretched to include within its ambit "volunteering" as there is a subtle but vital and clear distinction between the two. One can never be said to "volunteer" by "not objecting". Indeed, it is the case of the petitioner that in the event of the petitioner having really volunteered he would have had to fill and sign the form meant for volunteers and in paragraphs 5 of his affidavit solemnly affirmed on the 7th April 1994, the petitioner has, in terms, stated that after being moved to the new location he was asked to sign the format meant for volunteers which he refused to do. Further in paragraph 6 of the same affidavit he goes on to refer to "Formats prescribed by the Army Headquarters, New Delhi (MS policy dated 05.03.87 and 22.12.93) to be used for volunteers for postings is filed as Annexures 1, 2 and 3 with this affidavit." The annexures consist of formats of:

1. Willingness certificate
2. Adverse career certificate and
3. Medical certificate.

We cannot lose sight of the fact that the petitioner has not only made serious allegations[19] with regard to improper treatment meted out to the petitioner on the part of the fifth respondent but he has squarely placed it on record in a confidential communication addressed to the 5th respondent himself. We can also not lose sight of the fact that in the face of quite serious allegations in the petition, the 5th respondent has not chosen to come forward with an affidavit from himself either denying the correctness of the allegations or saying what he has to say about them. Even the counter affidavit filed on behalf of the respondent seeks to explain away the matter relating to the said letter Annexure 3 to the petition by suggesting that in the presence of Lt Col AK Singh the petitioner showed repentance for submitting complaint and respondent no. 5, in his magnanimity and also to give a fair chance to the petitioner to redeem his conduct, decided to condone this act and at the request of the petitioner the complaints, copy whereof is Annexure 3 to the petition, was torn. To support this the counter affidavit produces as Annexure CA 3 what purports to be a record of Capt Arun Kumar's interview with the CO on 25th of January, 1994, stated to have been written by Lt Col AK Singh. In the absence of any affidavit on the part of Lt Col AK Singh this document does not inspire much confidence, particularly because the normal and natural manner of recording such a thing, if the case put forward with regard to the oral withdrawal of allegations on the part of the petitioner and the letter dated 16th of January 1994, being torn after apology by the petitioner were true, would have been for the withdrawal

19 **Integrity.** Today Gen VK Singh is talking about his integrity. Where was his integrity when against serious allegations he failed to come forward with an affidavit himself either denying the correctness of my allegations regarding Siachen posting or saying what he had to say about those allegations.

of the said letter to be recorded by an endorsement made by the petitioner himself on the original letter dated 16th of January, 1994 at least stating that he had withdrawn the said letter (if not recording his purported apology/request). Against the aforesaid background of serious allegations made by the petitioner and the unsatisfactory manner of dealing with them in the counter affidavit (not forgetting the non-filing of an affidavit by respondent no. 5 and or by Lt Col AK Singh) and the unfair presentation of the picture by the fifth respondent in his aforequoted letter to the second respondent we find it appropriate to recording our disappointment if not, our downright distress at the state of affairs as we have found it. Further, against the background of tension between respondent no. 5 and the petitioner and the less than fair conduct on the part of the fifth respondent, the question about safety of the petitioner[20] from any vindictive action on the part of respondent no. 5 hereafter may raise itself almost naturally, but that is an area which does not fall within the domain of this court's inquiry and must be left to the mature handling, wisdom and foresight of the powers that be in the Indian Army. The learned advocate for the petitioner has presented a host of material to support the petitioner's plea that the petitioner could not have been posted (in terms of the policy of the Indian Army stated to have been clearly laid down) in the glacier region unless he had volunteered for the posting. We have not thought it necessary to refer to this material in the light of our having taken the view that we do not wish to interfere with this matter of posting in the Indian Army even though the material produced before us with regard to the petitioner's having "volunteered" has been less than convincing the precise or the more natural way of volunteering not having been found present in this case.

In the view that we have taken it will not be possible to grant any relief on this petition and, the circumstances, the petition must stand ordered to be dismissed. In view

20 **Harassment.** Since the court judgement prevented Col VK Singh from harassing me, he ensured Brig TS Gill exploits the situation (refer my letter to Brig TS Gill dated 06th June 2005 at page 126).

of the fact and circumstances of the case, however, there shall be no order as to costs of the petition.

July 28, 1994

Sd/

(Hon. AP Mishra, J.)
(Hon. MP Kenia, J.)

No Impact of HC Observations

It is really amazing to note that up the chain no senior officer of higher headquarters took note of the Allahabad High Court judgement wherein less than fair conduct was brought out on the part of Col VK Singh. It was pinpointed that in spite of serious allegations, Col VK Singh chose not to come on record to state the fact by means of filing a counter affidavit himself. Didn't Army and MOD take notice of the observations passed against him?

Letter of Maj Gen RS Taragi

The letter of the Col of the Regiment Maj Gen RS Taragi, referred to in the Allahabad HC judgement, is reproduced below:

Maj Gen RS Taragi
Col of Rajput Regt.
Tel. 7550
10021/RAJPUT/2

Headquarters
The College of Combat
Mhow (MP) 453441
31ST Dec. 1993

Dear Arun,

1. I am in receipt of your letter dated 24th Dec. 1993.
2. I agree with you that in spite of your being a non-volunteer, you have been posted to 23 RAJPUT for their glacier tenure. In the Regt we did not have very many volunteers, so I had left it to the MS Branch to select[21]

21 **Blatant Lie.** Col VK Singh said on receipt of the letter from the Col of the Regiment that he asked for volunteers in a discussion. However, this Col of the Regiment has something else to say. Col VK Singh had lied without realizing that in the court of law everything comes under close scrutiny.

the best and post them to 23 RAJPUT. You should be proud that you are amongst the chosen few. As a good Offr that you are, face the challenge and come out rich in experience. Serving in the Glacier is a man's job and a MAN that you are, I am confident you will give a good account of yourself.

3. I wish you the best and GOD SPEED, you will do well.

Sd/

Capt. Arun Kumar
2 RAJPUT
C/O 56 APO

Old Habits Die Hard

Let us have a look at some habits that define Gen VK Singh's personality:

- Right from Gen VK Singh's GC days of the IMA, it has been maintained that he is 'tactful'. A couple of senior officers in their reporting used the remark 'tactful' to describe GC VK Singh. Earning this remark so early in Army life and that too during training days at the IMA doesn't go down well for an officer and a gentleman. In Army parlance, this word is seen in a derogatory manner. In fact, over the years, Gen VK Singh has successfully honed all the traits that are normally considered negative but are so deeply ingrained in him.
- Age row has brought out in open his tactful/diplomatic mindset.
- He writes to COAS about accepting the date of birth issue in letter and spirit. True to his reputation, on NOO (not on original) writes to Defence Secretary also. In my case too, when he commented upon my 'volunteer posting', he sent the reply to Div HQ, Corps HQ, Cent Com and Army HQ on NOO with the sole intention that the higher HQs get carried away by his emotional note. (However, the Allahabad HC read the motive and brought it out

vividly). Bde HQ located in the same cantonment knew that my posting is the fallout of his wife's misconduct, which I stated verbally to Dy MS at MS Branch. Following this my posting was held in abeyance and comments were sought from Col VK Singh through proper channel.

- Very recently, he wrote to the Haryana Government to allot him a corner plot so that his ageing mother could benefit health-wise by staying in a three-side open house.

Gen VK Singh – Then and Now

Here is an analysis about the typical traits of Gen VK Singh.

Relied Upon!

Then: He got his Bn into a morass. (Interestingly, he said during Anna Hazare's fast that the nation is in a morass). His officers and families could not rely on him when he was expected to be "Man of The House." What a pity!

Many officers of the battalion stood by Col VK Singh during my posting row with him. They went out of their way to please him by lending all sorts of support with an aim to earn a good ACR. True to his reputation, Col VK Singh carried along with him all the ACR forms and later sent them by post after endorsing them. Few officers apprehended that they would be rated low in ACRs, and their apprehensions proved true and they did not make it to the next rank.

Now: In the age row, the defence ministry might be repenting as to why they did not take an affidavit from him. Perhaps the ministry thought a commitment given by an army officer is understood to be abided by – *pran jaye par vachan na jaye*. But it doesn't apply to him.

Attitude of Gratitude[22]

Then: As CO he should have taken measures to strengthen the battalion whose reputation was damaged by him earlier in the Kukrety case. Unfortunately, he took it to its lowest ebb because of his vindictive attitude.

Now: Weakening the same organisation which gave him the exalted position of its Chief. His lure for power (extra tenure) became an overriding issue for him which dented the Army reputation.

Comments: Media throughout was cautious while covering the Army Chief's age row. They hailed him as a fighter till, to everyone's surprise, he withdrew his petition when the moment of reckoning came. Today his criticism against media is totally uncalled for. At no stage, TV channels went for polls on "whether the Army Chief should resign or not?" Had a poll been conducted the result, probably, would have left General VK Singh red-faced. The media played a responsible role as they have the highest regard for the Indian Army as an institution. In spite of being fully aware of people's sentiments on the mess created by General VK Singh on his DOB., they chose not to sensationalise this issue for any TRP rating. They covered the age row in a very matured and responsible manner so as to ensure that the Army as an institution doesn't suffer due to anybody's personal ambitions.

Principled Stand

Then: He should have stood for his officers and SM when they were attached with different units in boxing incident.

Now: His age row was a stand which was purely individualistic. It had become an issue of the office of the

22 **Attitude towards Media**. Same media hailed General VK Singh as someone who would work for the betterment of Army. Media paid no head to wikicable. Media as late as 03rd Feb 2012 gave first round of victory to Gen. Unfortunately, on 03rd March 2012, Gen VK Singh states that the media was reporting obiter dicta in a highly exaggerated manner.

COAS and had inadvertently polarised the entire Army into followers of different camps, thereby undermining the basic fibre of Army. He would have earned appreciation had he stood up for professional growth of the Army. His claim on the DOB stood no ground as it was nearly dismissed by the Supreme Court in the very first hearing.

Backs Off

Then: I stood my ground firm and in spite of all rosy assurances I moved the court because I maintained throughout that I was not shirking from posting but protesting the manner in which Col VK Singh had lied to cover up his impropriety.

Now: Gen VK Singh had backed off from the commitment which he had given in writing on three occasions. A soldier remains committed to his stance irrespective of the consequences. As the Army Chief, he was expected to fight it out with MOD once he chose to move the court, but ironically, he meekly surrendered and lowered the image of this great institution. An active media has brought his intentions clearly out for a national debate. Is it about tenure or integrity? Reminds me of saying: "You can fool some people sometimes, but you cannot fool all the people all the time."

The picture which was painted all along that it was his animosity with Lt Gen Avadhesh Prakash which led to this age row. I for one believe that it was he who drew mileage from Sukhna scam as he used it to build up his own case throughout. In fact, Lt Gen Gangadharan and previous COAS bailed Gen VK Singh out by stating good things about him to MOD when his credentials and intentions were under scrutiny. These are the ethos and not the one which Gen VK Singh is displaying. Since 2006, right from his days as Corps Cdr to Army Commander to Army Chief all the precious time was wasted for personal issues.

Self Before Service

Then: He always thought about his career progression and manipulated his way to the top rank by filing many non-stat/stat complaints. Got postings and tenures to his liking and even the Commanders of his choice under whom he earned his ACR.

Now: His unsavoury act has dented the image of Army. The dignity of the Army Chief's office cannot be compromised! A vast majority of officers and men retire honourably and refrain from washing their dirty linen in public. For example, Lt Gen (Rtd) SK Sinha did not question the decision of the government and retired prematurely without any fuss.

A Liar?

Then: He made a laughing stock of himself by saying that I had volunteered for Siachen. Within no time, the Col of the Regiment sent a reply to me in writing stating "I agree with you that in spite of not being a volunteer you have been posted out."

Now: Fearing to be called a liar by his subordinates, he claimed that the commitment on his age was extracted from him. Was it a compulsion or expediency on his part? This irresponsible statement made him lose all credibility. Why did he not file a complaint then? Why did he give something in writing which he did not mean to follow?

Comments: General VK Singh took the plea that his troops would call him a liar if he doesn't go through the redressal system. This plea stood no logic. But by the same yardstick will the soldiers not call him 'coward' for not standing his ground in the Supreme Court?

I have throughout maintained that Col VK Singh had lied with respect to my posting as volunteer to Siachen, and it was proved beyond doubt by the Allahabad High Court judgement. During those days 'lie detector test' was not much in vogue or else he would have been subjected to that test.

Dramatics!

Then: The Allahabad HC judgement in my case says his letter to the then Army Chief ends in a dramatic manner. (Ref page 73) In the letter he wrote that I volunteered and then backed out - "how will men take it if one backtracks." Understandable, since schooldays Gen VK Singh has been part of drama club.

Now: The country witnessed for about a year the best display of his dramatics calibre. The drama began with an innocuous RTI query. Suitable leaks were given to the media to further his game plan. In spite of withdrawing his plea to the Supreme Court, he went on record stating that the objective of moving the court had been achieved. Is it true?

Unethical!

Then: All Army acts were violated to suit his move. He asked his subordinate to file counter affidavit on his behalf. Responding to my allegation that my posting is resultant of his wife's differences with my wife, the reply was sent up the channel under 2IC signature, not his. Interestingly, the reply was sent on NOO to higher formations to influence their decision.

Now: He earned all his promotions by accepting May 10, 1950 as his date of birth. Then he systematically tried to exploit the flaws in the system.

Gen VK Singh's Profile - A Misnomer

1. **Ranger Course:** Throughout his career, Gen VK Singh has gained enough mileage due to the Ranger Course which he had attended in the USA. Through reliable sources, it has been learnt that he had to undergo the course again to qualify. Someone rightly was denied a chance another time.

2. **Decorated Soldier:** He earned YSM as a Major. At this rank and service, an officer is expected to perform a gallantry

action and in all likelihood get rewarded for a brave action while facing bullets. Rarely, a Major earns a Seva Medal.

3. **YSM:** In the rank of Major one often hears an act of bravery because at this young age and service you interact closely with troops and lead by example in a challenging situation. Maj VK Singh must have carried out a challenging role beyond the realms of operational task. But one finds it difficult to digest that in a challenging and electrifying situation of IPKF operations in Sri Lanka how did he earn an award of this nature, when officers were being decorated with gallantry awards like Sena Medal, Kirti Chakra, etc.

4. **Commanding Officer Tenure:** This is the litmus test of leadership qualities. Many officers have faltered at this stage because one is responsible for one's troops advertent and inadvertent actions. Over here, he during his first six months of command had a mysterious death. The battalion did not fare well in any professional and sports competition. Nothing did the Bn achieve during its stay at LC. In peace location, the Bn got embroiled in an ugly fight with another Bn in a boxing final in his presence. Leadership par excellence! Earned a report after having been duly warned in writing by his seniors. Officers and SM got attached. The Bn on verge of being disbanded. But he made it to higher command to the dismay of the whole cantonment. Rarest of rare category achievement to rise to the rank of Army Chief.

5. **ACRs Redressal:** Never before in the history of the Indian Army an officer has made it to the rank of General by getting few complaints processed and obtaining redressal. If this was not enough, he chose to file a complaint again by almost making it to the record books (five hundred fifty pages of non-stat complaint).

6. **Field Tenures:** These tenures are tough and bring out the soldierly qualities, wherein one is tested for one's bravery as well as leadership traits. His field tenures are much less than what an officer with his service should have undergone.

7. **Leadership Qualities:** Wikicable says subordinates dislike him. Many incidents have testified this. Herein the difference between a good officer and a successful officer comes into play. A climber moves up the ladder irrespective of his command concerns. What a pity!

DP Kukrety Case: A Dark Chapter of VK Singh's Career

My battalion Kali Chindi witnessed one of the ugliest incidents in the history of the Indian Army. The case involved Maj VK Singh and Maj DP Kukrety who was gutsy and an upright officer known for his principled stand. A gold medalist from the Army Cadet College, Kukrety belonged to a family of three generations of Army officers and most of them have been decorated with gallantry awards including Shaurya Chakra. Soldiers literally worshipped him and stood by him as they looked up to him with awe and respect.

In the following paragraphs, misdemeanour of Maj VK Singh has been vividly brought out in Capt DP Kukrety's reply in his closing address to the reply submitted by the Prosecutor in GCM. It states:

I would like to state about the origin of the case.

Major VK Singh, ex 2 Rajput, presently posted in IMTRAT - BHUTAN was a perpetual offender who during my tenure of officiating Commanding Officer, committed following grave offences involving moral turpitude:

a. **Disobedience of lawful command.** This officer was sanctioned 7 days casual leave under very difficult circumstances when the sector had become tense and alive due to a border firing incident and this was the time when I needed sufficient of field officers with me. Incidentally, I was also short, or field officers at this particular time. Still, I sent Major VK Singh on 7 days casual leave and plonked myself in the FDLs during his absence. The officer instead of 7 days casual leave proceeded on 10 days casual leave.

b. Leaving Sr. No. 6 (Number of days leave applied for) and Sr. No. 8 (Number of days leave availed) of the casual leave application form blank. (This officer had already availed 12 days casual leave earlier from 04th Apr 78 to 16th Apr 78. He, therefore, wilfully left these serials blank. It was, therefore, a clear case of MORAL TURPITUDE).

c. Proceeded on 10 days casual leave, when Major VK Singh had already availed 12 days casual leave, thus exceeding his entitlement by 2 days.

d. **Having stated falsehoods.** (Perusal of abstract of evidence will clearly reveal that this officer resorted to falsehood in regard to Major AM Verma, (a junior officer, from whom he obtained a leave certificate for grant of 10 days casual leave), duty clerk and the duty runner.

These offences of Major VK Singh were of grave nature and could neither be acceptable nor could they be condoned in the interest of military discipline and good order which is the very edifice of our Army. Lt Col SN Verma therefore, forwarded Major VK Singh's case to Headquarters 93 Infantry Brigade along with the Abstract of evidence that was recorded against Major VK Singh. It stated:

(The following offences have been committed by Maj VK Singh – which was stated by ninteenth witness for Prosecution– IC13580Y Maj SN Verma:

a. Having obtained a leave certificate for 10 days, when only 7 days leave had been granted to him, through devious means by a junior officer;

b. Deliberately leaving Column 6 and 8 of the leave application form blank, and;

c. Having availed 2 days casual leave in excess of casual leave entitled to him.)

This officer had joined my unit as a youngster when I was a field officer. He had been professionally competent and also had been initially maintaining a disciplined life. He finally became a snob and a "Misguided Missile", after his marriage to the daughter of Mr. Vijay Pal Singh,

Deputy Speaker of Haryana Assembly. This person belonged to the Lok Dal when it had the majority in the Haryana Assembly. He (Mr. Vijay Pal Singh) finally defected from the Lok Dal and joined the folds of the Congress (I) on 17th Jan 1980 (*Indian Express* Chandigarh edition – of 18 Jan '80 - refers). He continued to be the Deputy Speaker of the Haryana Assembly as subsequently majority of the MLAs belonging to the ruling party, i.e., Lok Dal, defected and joined the Congress (I).

Mr. Vijay Pal Singh approached Gen Gurbachan Singh to extricate his son-in-law from this disciplinary case. Lt Gen Gurbachan Singh was too willing to bestow a favour on the Dy Speaker of Haryana Assembly, that, too, of the ruling party. He dare not miss such a golden opportunity which would later on serve him in good stead once he retires from the Army in Dec 1981 and even during his tenure of service in the Army.

Brigadier Kacker, Brigadier VP Bakshi, the then officiating GOC of 25 Infantry Division, and subsequently Major General Narender Singh who had some time in second week of Dec '78 joined back from leave, under the pressure and coercion of Lt Gen Gurbachan Singh, dropped the disciplinary case that was initiated by Lt Col Verma against Major VK Singh.

He goes on to say further at page 11:

On 01 Dec '78, Major VK Singh was remanded to Brigadier PN Kacker. At a later stage, on the same day, I was informed by the Adjutant that Brigadier Kacker wanted me in his office pertaining to the case of Maj VK Singh. Commander wanted me to narrate the whole episode since I had conducted the preliminary investigations and had submitted this to my Commanding Officer. I spoke in detail about the case and also apprised him of other numerous acts of omission and commission of Major VK Singh including the two that had been brought out by Major SN Verma in his deposition before the GCM.

The Commander stated that he would deal with this case himself. I told the Commander that he could not dispose off this disciplinary case as the officer held Major's rank which was out of his purview. He then told me that he would be forwarding Major VK Singh's case to the GOC. This transaction took place in the presence of Lt Col SN Verma.

On 08 Dec '78, Major VK Singh spoke to Capt VK Pillai, who was then in the process of handing over the duties of Adjutant to Capt SS Yadav, and enquired from him as to who was holding the Imprest Account and whether the ATG bills have been sorted out.

He also submitted two superfluous points for the Mess Meeting which was to be held shortly. Capt VK Pillai spoke to me and to Lt Col SN Verma about these. It was clear that this officer wanted to threaten and blackmail me and my Commanding Officer with a view to deter us from proceeding with his disciplinary case.

During the last week of Nov '78 and first week of Dec '78, the 2 Rajput Base exchange received 3 to 4 calls from Mr Vijay Pal Singh, the Dy Speaker of Haryana Assembly. Major VK Singh was informed by his wife that her father had approached Lt Gen Gurbachan Singh, the Army Commander who had assured her father to do the needful.

On 06 Dec '78 evening, I was called by my CO. He told me that Brigadier YP Bakshi officiating GOC and Lt Col Kuttappa had told the Commander that there was no prima facie case existing against Major VK Singh. He further said that 4 of our officers have also been implicated including me.

I therefore sought, a personal interview of the Commander on 04 Dec 78 and had a prolonged discussion with him. I apprised him of the latest telephonic conversations of Major VK Singh with Capt Pillai and enjoined on him not to drop the case of Major VK Singh.

I also apprised the Commander that I had been dealing with the offenders, especially, those who had been wilfully committing offences, without any compassion and that he could ask for the offence register from 2 Rajput. The Commander apparentely posed to be unmoved. I also told the Commander that Lt Col Verma, too, was strict in dealing with the offenders.

I then categorically told the Commander that if there is no prima facie case existing against Major VK Singh, then in that case I should be charged for making a false accusation against an officer. If this was not done then the Commander would have to attach me to any other unit.

After sometime, around 1145 hrs, the same day when my Commanding Officer and I were sitting in Major Preet Pal Singh's office, Major Preet Pal Singh (DAA and QMG) brought an open - written apology - letter from Major VK Singh and handed it to Lt Col Verma. Major VK Singh at that time was sitting with Major Mehta, Brigade Major, in the latter's office. This was in response to Lt Col Verma's response mode to the Commander on 01 Dec '78 that this officer Major VK Singh had not even had the decency of apologising orally. Lt Col Verma showed me the letter, I retorted that it was a toilet paper.

On 10 Dec '78, Capt AK Singh confided in me that all the telephonic conversations that were being done between the Commanding Officer, the 2IC and Adjutant were being heard by Major VK Singh who was then at "DURGA". This officer was with Major VK Singh for a couple of days prior to leaving on 12 days casual leave wef 12 Dec 78 to 23 Dec '78. All these actions of Major VK Singh convinced me that this individual was INCORRIGIBLE. I apprised my Commanding Officer about this.

....

And it contained many pages of facts regarding misdemeanour about Major VK Singh.

(In para 3 of the address the prosecutor had stated that this is perhaps a rare example in a criminal trial where the accused persons have been consistently refusing to defend themselves.)

As prosecution witness number 19, Maj SN Verma (Ex-CO 2 Rajput) in GCM proceeding wherein, Brig Choudhari Vijay Kumar was the presiding officer, goes on to state after having been duly affirmed (page 176, para 4) that "the next day I was summoned to HQ 25 Inf Div alongwith Maj VK Singh. I was first called by the GOC in the presence of the Brigade Commander. The GOC asked me how I wanted Maj VK Singh's case to be dealt with. I told him that all the documents including papers for the summary disposal of the case were with him. He insisted that as Commanding Officer I should give my opinion. I told him that he should be tried under the provisions of Army Act Section 84, particularly when this offence is viewed in the backdrop of his earlier two offences - one of which was for disobedience of orders in that he did not carryout the assigned task and being improperly turned out during the visit of the Col of the regiment and the second one was for bartering rum, the troops ration, for kerosene oil."

This statement should be read in conjunction with the under mentioned confidential letter written by the CO regarding discipline and misconduct of Major VK Singh. This letter will provide readers with an insight about manipulative attitude of Major VK Singh. It is reproduced as under:

Note: In my case when Gen VK Singh approached the Army Chief he wanted the sanctity of the institution of Commanding Officer to be maintained. Earlier, he tarnished the institution of CO by his own conduct and today he has done collateral damage to the institution of Army Chief.

CONFIDENTIAL

2 RAJPUT
C/O 56 APO
19 Nov. 78

3200 / 31 / A (C)
Brig P.N. Kacker, SC, VSM,
Cdr. 93 Inf. Bde.

DISCIPLINE OFFRS

1. Ref. our tele and verbal conversation of 16 and 17 Nov '78 respectively.
2. Prior to proceeding on my annual leave on 14th October '78, I had verbally sanctioned seven days casual leave to IC 24137W Maj VK Singh. This was conveyed to IC 14561A Maj DP Kukrety, my 2IC, who was officiating in my absence.
3. On my return from annual leave, I was officially apprised by my 2IC that Maj VK Singh although sanctioned seven days casual leave proceeded on ten days casual leave. He informed that acts of omission had been committed by Maj VK Singh, IC 27038N Maj AM Verma and SS 27018A Capt VK Pillai. A copy of the report submitted by my 2IC after his having carried out a detailed investigation has already been handed over to you for your perusal.
4. The case has been further investigated by me and is being reported to you in the succeeding paras.
5. On 14th Oct '78 (after my dep. on my annual leave), due to a border firing incident in the 8 Kumaon Def. Area the sector became tense and, therefore, due to the changed op sit, Maj DP Kukrety the Offg. CO then, informed Maj VK Singh that it will not be possible for him to proceed on casual leave as planned and that he would reconsider his being sanctioned casual leave later when the op sit improved. On 16 Oct '78, the Offg CO accordingly informed Maj VK Singh that he may proceed on seven days casual leave with effect from 17th October '78. This

information was personally passed by the Offg CO to Maj VK Singh twice on the same day, i.e. 16 October '78. This information (viz sanctioning of seven days casual leave to Maj VK Singh from 17 Oct '78) was also personally conveyed by the Offg CO to Capt VK Pillai, the Adjt, the same day.

6. The Adjt accordingly asked the Offg Head Clk (Nk/Clk Rajendra Pal Singh) to take out a set of leave application forms as Maj VK Singh was to proceed on seven days casual leave. Apparently as the major portion of the "A" office had been shifted to the Tac HQ and the leave application forms were not available, the Adjt did not give instructions to the Offg. Head Clerk to prepare a leave certificate at that juncture. Later, however, the Adjt contacted the BHM (Hav Ravinder Singh) from the Tac HQ on telephone and gave instructions to him to get the casual leave certificate typed by the duty clerk for grant of ten days casual leave.

7. Meanwhile, knowing that the Adjutant may not be available in the Adm. Base due to the shifting of the "A" office on 16 Oct '78, Maj DP Kukrety had passed clear instructions to Maj AM Verma, (who was to stay in the Adm Base), to sign Maj VK Singh's casual leave certificate, granting him seven days casual leave.

8. Maj VK Singh is reported to have arrived in the Adm. Base from his picquet around 1900 hrs on 16th October 1978. The moment the Offr arrived from his picquet, even before going to his room/Offrs' Mess, the Offr. was apparently aware that he was proceeding on ten days casual leave. The interrogation of the Duty Runner (Sep. Rajpal) and the statement of the Duty Clk (Nk/Clk Mohan Das) corroborating the conversation between the Duty Runner and Maj VK Singh (as revealed by the Duty Runner), cleary leads one to believe so. It also transpired that on instructions from the Duty Clerk, the Duty Runner reported to Maj VK Singh and brought the details of leave (with dates of leave with effect from 17th October to 26th October 1978) and the details of form D required (both of which were written by Maj VK Singh in

his own handwriting on a piece of paper), and handed it over to the Duty Clk (Nk/Clk Mohan Das).

9. Although Capt VK Pillai denies having told Maj VK Singh about the grant of ten days casual leave, it is not understood how the Adjt personally conveyed to the BHM (Hav Ravinder Singh) regarding the preparation of a leave certificate for grant of ten days casual leave to the officer (Maj VK Singh) which was contrary to the orders given by Maj DP Kukrety, the Offg. CO then. It is relevant to put out here that before the Adjt conveyed this to the GHM, the duty Clk had already obtained the details of casual leave to be granted from the Offr (Maj VK Singh) himself, in his own hand writing.

10. Notwithstanding, whether or not Maj VK Singh was earlier aware of his having been granted ten days casual leave, the moment there arose a doubt in his mind (whether he had been granted seven days or ten days casual leave) it was his bounden duty to personally confirm from the Offg. CO or the Adjt and clarify this doubt, particularly so, when he was fully aware of the circumstances in which he was being granted seven days casual leave. More so, when the Offg. CO had personally conveyed to him on the same day that he could proceed on seven days casual leave commencing from 17th October 1978. Although the Offr. admits that a doubt existed (para 6 of his explanation refers), yet the Offr failed to seek clarification. The Offr's statement that he tried to contact the Offg. CO and the Adjt to clarify the doubt does not appear to be true, as both (the Offg. CO and the Adjutant) were all along present in the Ops. Room/residence (Tac HQ). In any case from approximately 2000 hrs on 16 Oct '78 (the time Maj VK Singh claims to have contacted the Adjutant or the Offg CO) to 0400 hrs on 17th October, '78 (the time the officer left the Adm Base) a period of nearly eight hrs, is considered more than adequate for Maj VK Singh to have contacted the Offg. CO or the Adjt on phone. Besides this unbecoming conduct, when asked to explain the circumstances under which he proceeded on ten days casual leave, the Offr has been impertinent

and has made assumptions to suit his own convenience in his written explanation.

11. The leave certificate granting the Offr ten days casual leave was signed by Maj AM Verma. This was again contrary to the Offg. CO's orders and at no stage clarification was sought, either from the Offg. CO or the Adjt.

12. In addition to the above, it is on record that Maj VK Singh has already availed 12 days casual leave w.e.f. 04 Apr to 15 April '78. A perusal of the Offr's leave application will reveal that the Offr has deliberately chosen to leave paras 6 and 8 blank for reasons best known to him. The Offr. disregarded the fact that he had already availed 12 days casual leave and acted in a most irresponsible and immature manner to have proceeded on ten days casual leave, thereby exceeding his entitlement by two days. An Offr of Maj VK Singh's seniority should have known better. Assuming for a moment that a casual leave certificate was issued to him for availing ten days casual leave inadvertently, with his service and experience he should have pointed out the fact to the Adjt or Maj AM Verma (who signed his leave certificate) that he had already availed 12 days casual leave and not more than eight days casual leave could be entitled to him.

13. Both Maj AM Verma and Capt VK Pillai are also guilty of omissions (though to a lesser degree). Capt. VK Pillai is being relieved of the appt. of Adjut, in addition both Maj AM Verma and Capt VK Pillai are being issued with written warnings for their irresponsible actions.

14. Maj VK Singh has been guilty of deliberately committing acts of omission of a nature, which in the interest of service is not acceptable as also cannot be condoned. A prima facie case exists against this Offr. The Offr is chargeable under the following offences:

    (a) AA Sec 41 (I) - Disobedience to a superior Offr.

    (b) AA Sec 42 (a) - Neglecting to obey a gen order.

    (c) AA Sec 63 - An act/omission prejudicial to good order and mil discipline.

    (d) AA Sec 45 - Unbecoming conduct.

15. It will not be out of place to mention here that Maj VK Singh had been admonished by me for being improperly turned out, as also for not having carried out the duties assigned to him satisfactorily, during the Col of the Regt's visit to the unit of 22 Sep '78. On the second occasion[23] this Offr was guilty of a deliberate Adm omission/lapse, in that, the procedure adopted by the Offr in his sub unit for receipt of stores was highly incorrect and illegal, and had it not been detected in time it would have tantamounted to misappropriation of Govt. property. For this the Offr was officially marched up and warned by me.

16. In spite of earlier admonishment and warning as also my personal counselling from time to time, this Offr has shown no improvement and has now committed offences which are unpardonable. I have, therefore, no option but to remand him to you for further necessary disciplinary action.

19 Nov. 1978

Sd/- SN Verma
Lt Col

Fallout of Kukrety–Singh Duel

DP Kukrety stood his ground and the whole issue went out of hand when Maj VK Singh moved out on permanent posting to IMTRAT (Bhutan). First time ever, the Bde Cdr as reliably learnt signed the movement order for Maj VK Singh as none else signed in the unit.

The court of inquiry in its findings and opinion indicted HQ 25 Inf Div. Maj Gen Narendra Singh and Brig Kacker. In para 8 of its findings, the court of inquiry made the following observations about HQ 25 Inf. Div:

"It is outside the scope of this court to comment on the legality and rationale of the action taken by HQ 25 Inf Div. However we have following observations to make:

---

23 **Second Offence.** It was for bartering rum, the troops ration, for kerosene oil. About this offence Ex-CO made a mention to the GOC and said it be viewed seriously against the present offence concerning casual leave.

- Maj VK Singh, having become aware that a confusion was prevailing about the number of days for which his leave was sanctioned did not take enough care to clarify it.
- Major VK Singh proceeded on 10 days casual leave when he had already availed 12 days casual leave thus exceeding his entitlement by 2 days.

At Annexue "E" the findings of the Court of Enquiry were:

2 Rajput had preferred four charges against Maj VK Singh on 1 Dec '78 as follows:

- Disobedience of lawful command in that he proceeded on 10 days casual leave against a sanction of 7 days by the Offg. CO.
- Leaving ser 6 (Number of days applied for) and ser 8 (Number of days leave available) of the casual leave application form blank.
- Proceeded on 10 days casual leave, when Maj VK Singh had already availed 12 days casual leave, thus exceeding his entitlement by 2 days.
- Having stated falsehoods during investigations.

It also states that:

On 16 Dec '78, on return from Div HQs the state of mind of Lt Col SN Verma was as follows:

- The Bde Cdr had been trying to pressurise him in dropping the case.
- He had taken Maj VK Singh to the GOC on a disciplinary matter, but instead he had been put in the dock.
- Maj VK Singh had been very leniently dealt with
- Three other Offrs had also been indicted for adm lapses.

(As is evident from the above, the whole issue revolved around a frivolous issue of casual leave of Maj VK Singh. Had Maj VK Singh apologised, the whole issue would have not flared up to such an extent. Adding to the fire was the lenient punishment of displeasure awarded by the GOC, (not to be recorded) and thereafter Maj VK Singh moving out on posting to IMTRAT, Bhutan).

Lastly as prosecution witness number 23 – IC 12403M Lt Col IJ Chanda CO 2/3 GR also states that he was told that Maj DP Kukrety was aware of some telephonic conversation between Maj VK Singh and Mrs VK Singh. This also finds reference in para 258(j) of the court of inquiry proceedings. Reproduced:

"258...

(j) Maj Kukrety also stated that he was aware of a telephonic conversation between Maj VK Singh and his wife wherein his wife informed Maj VK Singh that her (Mrs VK Singh's) father had spoken to the Army Commander and that everything would be sorted out. Now as Maj Kukrety put it "It is between Gen Gurbachan Singh and Sri Ramchandra Ji" or words to that effect. Maj Kukrety said that the General Officer Commanding and the Brigade Commander were under pressure from higher Headquarter on this account."

(In the Kukrety case description, I have purposely kept myself within a limit so as not to bring out certain actions consequent to Maj VK Singh's moving out on posting to IMTRAT on 20th Dec 1978 as this would not be good for the image of the Indian Army in general and my battalion in particular. I am wary of the fact that some authors tend to transgress the ethical boundary to sensationalise issues. But I refrain from doing so as my sole aim is to bring out misconduct on the part of Gen VK Singh.

This ugly incident was outcome of Maj VK Singh's ego. An apology from Maj VK Singh to Maj DP Kukrety would have put to rest the whole incident. CO and 2IC were right in their tough stance as they had set high discipline standards regarding leave in the unit for the jawans. The matter was viewed seriously by the CO as he considerd Maj VK Singh action as stepping out of the shoe especially against the backdrop of his previous offence on moral turpitude. The matter flared up when Maj VK Singh asked for his father-in-law help to bail him out. Maj DP Kukrety got infuriated on learning that unwanted political interference is being sought for such a trivial issue wherein officer should have moral courage to own up the mistake.

Sadly, Maj DP Kukrety was levelled with a serious charge. An officer who had taken up principled stand also earned praise from the prosecutor of GCM in para three of the address that 'this is perhaps a rare example in a criminal trial where the accused persons have been consistenly refusing to defend themselves'.

Basic Traits Never Change

1. **1965:** According to Gen VK Singh, his teacher filled up the UPSC form wrongly by stating silly reasons.
2. **1969:** Fills up IMA Dossier in own handwriting. DOB filled up as 1950. States that since it was to be in consonance with the UPSC form, hence he filled his DOB as 1950. Pertinent to mention that the dossier remains with the IMA itself, hence this logic holds no ground.

(There is a column in the dossier which says FOR USE IN ARMY HQ – was this verification of DOB not for AGs Branch. So rightfully AG should maintain 1950 and not 1951 as claimed by him).

3. **1970:** In his pen picture at more than two places by his reporting officers, it has been mentioned that gentleman Cadet VK Singh is "tactful". (No soldier likes to be associated with this term.)
4. **1978:** Batallion underwent humiliation and was on the verge of being disbanded. The following traits of Gen VK Singh came to the fore:

   a. **Moral Turpitude** - Leaving certain columns unfilled in leave application form speaks about his manipulative nature. Primarily, his aim was to mislead and derive maximum benefit for himself.

b. **Unbecoming Conduct** – One doesn't quote one's juniors and relies on a Havildar to give silly excuses as he gave in his defence for 10 days casual leave.

c. **Absent without Leave** – A serious offence in the Army. Soldiers get 14 days rigorous imprisonment for this offence. Rightly so, CO and 2IC wanted officers also to be dealt severely on this count. Was it not a case of break in service?

d. **Wife's Influence** – Amply clear from the log message book of the unit that he consistently spoke to his wife to bail him out of this precarious situation. Resultant of which he was let off with a lenient punishment of "Displeasure" (Not to be recorded).

e. **Self before Battalion** – In the end, it was the battalion which suffered the most. It was moved out from one operational area to another and was on the brink of being disbanded.

5. **1994**

a. **Misdemeanour** – Col VK Singh ill-treated myself on both the counts, i.e. professionally and personally. In spite of being the Commanding Officer of the battalion, he allowed his wife to interfere in the unit's administrative affairs. A CO is a pillar of strength and source of inspiration for his jawans.

b. **Impropriety** – He misused govt. property which I brought out in my letter dated 16th Jan 1994. He misused his office and position by asking a junior officer to sign the counter affidavit in the Allahabad High Court wherein he should have himself done it being respondent No. 5.

c. **Misuse of MCN** – He misused two military credit notes for getting gensets from Agra to Faizabad in the second week of January 1994 by sending Havildar Sishupal Singh along with another sepoy on two occasions. It was a Court Martial offence which I brought out in my non-statutory complaint of 1994.

d. **Making use of the System** – In desperation, he wrote to the then COAS to post me out of the battalion by writing to him emotionally. The Allahabad High Court saw through his intentions and brought it out vividly in their observations. Also he gave comment on the NOO when asked to verify about his wife's differences with my wife in a bid to post me out. The sole reason was to apprise higher headquarters without letting Bde. HQ know about the reply. Same he did later on when he wrote to Defence Secretary on NOO while writing to COAS, Gen Deepak Kapoor about his commitment on DOB.

e. **Failure of Command** – In his presence troops of the battalion picked up a fist fight with troops of 7 Kumaon. Resultant of which two Company Commanders and SM got attached to different units and he went for higher command.

6. 2012

a. **Moral Courage** – General VK Singh made a mockery of the whole system and ridiculed the institution by stating that he gave all the three commitments on DOB under coercion. People rightly asked was not that the time to move a statutory complaint for seeking justice and not after having obtained rank and then asking for extension of tenure.

Yes, he is correct to state that TV commentators drew parallels to Gen KS Thimmaya. But, Gen Thimmaya had the moral courage to put up his resignation, wherein, in your case in spite of the same TV commentators who supported your cause all throughout were aghast to learn that you do not intend to resign in spite of 10th Feb SC hearing. Sad!

b. Two 'General Hoots' for the 'Self Before Service' Motto – The famous Chetwode saying laid to rest!!! A leading English magazine came out with the front page cover as "Self before Service" while reporting on the issue of Gen VK Singh DOB. For the first time a soldier appeared on a cover story for wrong reasons.

c. **Unprecedented Acts** - For the first time ever, the Army Chief files a statutory complaint and moves the court. Every soldier was of a singular opinion that Gen VK Singh should have resigned first and then moved the court for seeking "so called" justice.

d. **Smear Campaign** - An innocuous RTI; seeking opinion from three retired Chief Justices of India on DOB, etc. He admonished previous Chiefs and made the whole world believe that he had become victim of circumstances mainly by previous COAS. It was all part of his smear campaign. Of late, he has started blaming everyone (left, right and centre) including serving officers, forgetting that 'people who stay in glass houses do not throw stones at others'. No one had any vested interest when he filled up his IMA dossier in 1969 as his DOB as 1950. Such things behove a politician and not a soldier. Imagine 37 MPs reaching out to PM for intervening in DOB case. Parliament question being raised to clarify his date of retirement. Ex CM of a state coming out in open to support his cause. Opposition Parties taking a dig at the government on the age row - never before this great institution has witnessed so much of political attention.

e. **Matter of Honour** - Had it been a matter of his honour as was made out to be then 10th Feb 2012 should have been the last day in the office for Gen VK Singh. It was the day when he threw the towel in the DOB case. A soldier is known for sticking to his stand irrespective of the consequences. Reminds of the famous couplet "Honour and shame from no condition rise; Act well your part, there all the honour lies". Read it in conjunction with "A delicacy of honour that is sensitive to shame".

Army Chief needs to look inwards first, rather than accuse others. A cadet going back on his word in the training academy may even be relegated for lack of OLQ (officer like qualities). He did not even think twice before stating that he informed the Defence Minister, regarding the bribery, thereby, putting him in a tight position, especially when Mr. Antony's conduct was more than graceful in his DOB case.

The bribe offer issue has once again reiterated that General VK Singh lacks courage. Had he gone ahead to proceed officially with the person who had offered him the bribe, he would have set an unprecedented example of bravery and courage. But as he had always put 'self before service,' hence he went for other unprecedented acts. It will be better if he comes out with some strong evidence or else people on civvie street will be compelled to label him as ordinary man who is casting aspersion purely out of disgruntlement and frustration. He is not genuine in his intent, neither in his words nor action.

He cannot be offered to play politics with the security of the nation as he writes to PM to pass "suitable directions to enhance the preparedness of the Army". He kept the vital issues related to Army modernisation on the back burner and wasted his tenure in fighting his unwarranted and out of place issue regarding DOB. Sooner or later a balance sheet of his career will reveal that he did precious little since his tenure of Corps Commander. As Divisional Commander he must have noticed deficiencies of bullet proof jackets; during his Corps Commander stint he would have taken note of deficiencies with armoured divisions and during his tenure as Army Commander he would have definitely observed war preparedness with China. Did he ever bring out anything alarming to the notice of his superiors? Then, why now??

On 30th March 2012, a leading TV News Channel ran the news as 'General's Retreat'. Gen VK Singh comes out with another conciliatory statement that one should be aware of rogue elements who are creating a schism between Army and Government. A soldier is known for taking issues to its logical end.

He has made the Army a mean of gossip and ridicule by his unsavory conduct. The media has given an opportunity to all and sundry to comment on every matter which was never the case earlier. **Unfortunate**!

Chapter 4

24 Carat Impropriety

After my posting to NSG was cancelled in 'organisational interest', I was looking forward to another physically demanding tenure. And, when I received my posting order to HQ SFF, my joy knew no bounds. Like my earlier tenures elsewhere, I went beyond the call of duty during my HQ SFF posting. I gave exemplary performances, resultant of which I was posted at their prestigious academy within a year.

I undertook each opportunity as a challenge, and within a few months I was entrusted with the charge of the rock climbing school. I had the sole privilege of briefing and conducting all VVIPs during their visit to HQ 22 Est. The HQ SFF tenure provided me an opportunity to give vent to my urge for innovativeness. I humbly submit that I was the architect of few projects which were appreciated by one and all.

The real honour came in when I was handpicked by the IG to carry out purchases for revamping the rock climbing school. Being an infantry officer, I found my selection strange. In my new role, I made purchases after detailed market survey leading to large savings. This served as a prelude to purchases which were to be made after the Kargil conflict. I was the obvious choice.

Unaware of vested interests I continued with the same zeal and vigour as part of the board of officers appointed for the purchase of mountaineering equipment. Slowly senior officers started showing their true Colours. I was intrigued by the apparent change in their behaviour. However, unmindful of their hidden agenda, I moved on with guards down and in turn I paid a heavy penalty. Gist of my stat complaint says it all. (Refer to page 44)

Officers with unquestionable integrity are posted to SFF. It is logical to conclude that the head of the institution/ organisation will be a man of impeccable integrity. But retired Brigadier Uban rose to the rank of IG SFF in a calculated manner. Generally, a serving Maj Gen occupies the coveted post of Inspector General SFF. Therefore, despite being a retired Brigadier, Uban's becoming the IG could not have been anything but pure manipulation.

Kargil Conflict - A Godsent for the Corrupt

IG Uban exploited the Kargil conflict to the hilt. Purchases made after the Kargil conflict, that is w.e.f. July '99, were phenomenal. All purchases were made without assessing proper requirement and utility of the items being purchased. IG Uban made trips abroad along with his wife and made most of the Kargil conflict. As regards mountaineering equipment, at the first place the equipment was not required and secondly there was no place to carry out mountaineering training at some of the 8 locations mentioned for purchases. I was initially part of the board of officers for the purchases to be made based on my past negotiating skills. But, when I expressed my concern regarding the method employed to procure stores, my name was conveniently replaced by IC51707 Capt Kulkarni Vikrant (who signed on the dotted line). The Presiding Officer, Lt Col Pankaj Awasthi and IC 52210 Capt SK Dutta names continued to be there. My tough stance almost got the purchase order cancelled but that was not to be. Otherwise, I would not have been compelled to bring to the notice of the readers how the precious tax payers' money was squandered by the powers that are with SFF.

My following letter will give the readers an insight into the state of affairs at SFF:

CONFIDENTIAL

IC 48868A
Maj Arun Kumar

SFF Academy
C/O 56 APO

AK/PERS/48368

13 Dec 99

Sir,

1. Ref my visit to your office on 02 Dec '99 at 1230 hrs.
2. I had come to you to discuss certain things. When I had put across the facts and sought certain clarifications, then you came out with the excuse that you are very busy with the PD's visit and once the visit is over you will discuss and clarify. But your departure on AL till first week of Feb gave me an indication that you are reluctant to discuss what you promised as you are aware that I will be posted out by January '99.
3. In the midst of my prep for my exam, I decided to initially shelve the entire thing for the time being and discuss it later. I was not at peace with myself and hence was compelled to write to you.

4. Sir, one can understand the perks and privileges that go with the appointment, like your shifting of computer and TV to your residence. You took personal interest in acquiring straight dialing facility in your room from Sig coy only with a view to dispense with your civ tele connection. This tele is now the only means of your comn with your family at Dehradun, and is used extensively. Your actions are motivated and manipulated to purely suit your personal interest in the garb of organisational interest. But such privileges behove only when genuine concern for the organisation is also displayed. At no stage you took any classes, never ever you were present during conduct of SI or Cdr test. No exercise was conducted by the Academy and neither was any insp carried out by you to take stock of the things on grnd. Your personal involvement was conspicuous by its absence.

5. Your leaning towards anybody is always with a selfish desire. The affiliations remains till it's of relevance to you and thereafter you drop it as a hot brick. A case in point is that you never cared to visit ailing Col Rana at RandR Hospital at Delhi, while you were in Delhi on Temp Duty. You were a totally transformed man in your attitude and actions after your ACR was rewritten for better in sharp contrast to your outlook exhibited during the sainik sammelan and dining out of Col HV Singh, the previous day.

6. It was amazing to know that an Offr of your rk and stature will stoop so low to conspire with an NCO. The regmt was to forge the bonafide documents in respect of Sep Laxman Singh whom you got posted from HQ 22 Est on the pretext of trg recruit (enhanced intake) as he was a qualified instr on PT course. In carrying out his mov the Academy had to post a Hav to HQ 22 Est in lieu, but Sep Laxman Singh was posted and ultimately emp as your sahayak at SF accn. It smacks of cunningness and shrewdness, more, if viewed in entirety. A host of such issues are there.

7. In my earlier correspondence*, I had highlighted about your intention in recommending the proposals for

procurement of rock climbing eqpt. Your unprecedented enthusiasm in dealing with supplier evoked suspicion in everyone's mind. You were extremely selective in calling for quotation and made your intentions obvious during opening of tenders on 04 Oct '99. The revealing documents have been purposefully removed / destroyed to give semblance of orderliness. Leave aside a thorough examination even a cursory glance will est the irregularity. Your inner-self is a witness to the facts about your hush-hush handling. I am sure at all the time these must be at the back of your mind and to cover up you must have thought of keeping IG in picture. But I am more than confident that the briefings on the subject would have been selective and half baked.

8. It is widely known that IG is a man of unquestionable integrity. Undoubtedly, he has done a lot for the uplift-ment of this org and his untiring efforts have given a face-lift to this force but your action are in contrast with his accomplishments. He will be astonished to learn about such betrayal of confidence.

9. Presumably, this piquant situation has been created because of your vested interests. Hence, now I am sure a man with your ambition will make necessary amends.

Sd/

Lt Col Pankaj Awasthi, SM***
SFF Academy
C/O HQ Est 22
C/O 56 APO

Gross Irregularity in Purchases of Mountaineering Equipment

I find it difficult to comprehend that how an elite organisation can make purchases by fraudulent means. In case of HQ SFF, there was neither requirement nor the place for much of the mountaineering equipment that was bought. Even the relevance of other purchases during that time, especially the signal equipment, merits scrutiny.

On the one hand, I through negotiations with the suppliers succeeded in bringing approx 50 per cent reduction in the per metre price of two types of ropes (climbing and rappelling). On the other hand, some officers made purchases by incorrect means. Their only agenda was to exploit in the garb of the Kargil conflict. Before I could do anything to check their dubious plans, I was sidelined. However, I brought the wrong doings to the notice of my seniors, resultant of which the whole tender process for procuring mountaineering equipment was cancelled. But it was reordered when one dealer, Mr Surinder of STIKAGE from Delhi, threatened the HQ SFF to move the court. The extracts from my non-stat complaint will provide an insight into the murky deal (Refer page 45)

Fait accomplai!

All officers posted at SFF Academy were privy to the manipulation done to make the fraudulent purchases. Some of the glaring irregularities in the procurement of mountaineering equipment are listed below:

(a) The rope quotation was called from only one wholesaler and all other contenders were retailers — an example of sheer manipulation. Hence, automatically the rope contract was to go to this wholesaler. The price negotiation with the wholesaler led to price reduction by only a few paisa per meter. However for the same rope, I had earlier brought down the price by nearly 50% – from Rs 22 per metre to Rs 13.

(b) The shortlisting of firms for various stores was not in order for various stores. On 06 Dec 1999 Lt Col Pachory of Mahar Regiment placed on record in writing certain anomalies in the board proceedings and with respect to shortlisting. This was evident from the fact that for both type of ropes (climbing and rapelling), quotations were asked from only one wholesaler ie, Motilal Duli Chand (Pvt) Ltd.

(c) Mr Surinder of STIKAGE (Delhi) wrote that he was shocked and hurt to learn about the cancellation of the tender process for the mountaineering equipment. He threatened to recover loss through legal means if the original supply order was not restored within 10 days. Then yielding to Mr Surinder's threat, the supply order was reissued.

(d) IG Uban got included all the critical equipment in the list of items to be procured from the IMF, but he purposely omitted crampons which were bought from Mr Jatin Anand of Malik Chand Kishan Lal and Co, Dehradun. This Dehradun dealer was a favourite of Lt Col P Awasthi. Only 80 crampons at Rs 2500 per pair (reduced to Rs 2425 following the efforts of PNC) were bought from Malik Chand and Co as they had only this quantity in their stock. In a classic example of manipulation, the requirement of crampons was shown only as 80 in the reserve category. Like other items which were critical for the safety and security of personnel, crampons should also have been bought from the IMF which would have provided them duty-free. IG Uban and Col Pankaj Awasthi had no answer to this blatant irregularity, and when you pointed out this in your statutory complaint, their was no answer.

(e) If an officer of the IG rank takes personal interest in purchases then there could be only one motive and that could be a major vice. That's the reason my DO to him went unreplied. The DO reads:

Dear Sir,

1. I had informed Fiama about the change in your departure schedule at about 1400 hrs and I am sure the tpt would have reached in time.

2. Sir, I am at loss of words to express my gratitude for the assurance that you gave me about everything being

sorted out regarding my CR. I am happy that as the head of the family you were generous and kind enough to understand that a minor family discord should not be the end of career for an Offr whom you had personally watched from close quarters. On professional account you had seen me more than the Commandant. Sir, regarding the domestic problem, I assure you that it was a trivial issue much within the limits of normal day-to-day affair between husband and wife, which was blown out of proportions and projected to Commandant by Col Awasthi. I could not sense the timing of it, still I promised/assured Comdt of proper conduct. Today, after meeting you personally, I am overjoyed and I promise you that I will be more than careful about it in near future, as I may not be fortunate enough again to have someone as considerate and understanding as you. A microscopic view of the complete affair reveals that the date of the incidence as mentioned is the day of "Karva Chauth", wherein my wife observes fast and prays for my longevity and prosperity.

3. Due to change in your departure schedule, I in a hurry without realising and by mistake handed you over two copies of the same letter i.e. DEPRIVATION OF BONA FIDE DUTY Dt. 19 Feb 2000, that was written to Col APS Pakianathan, Cdr SFF Academy, wherein I wanted to hand over letter No AK/Pers/48368 dt. 13 Dec. '99. Hence, I am enclosing a photocopy of the letter and despatching it imdt by a private courier. Even the letter dt. 18 Nov '99 was addressed to Lt Col Pankaj Awasthi. I also handed over a set of documents to Col Pakianathan before leaving the Academy, which will conclusively est the impropriety on conduct of Col Awasthi. I became a victim of circumstances, but after meeting you now I realise that meeting you was purely coincidental and definitely a God sent opportunity. Now I am at peace with myself and your assurance will do me and my family lot of good. I am going to prepare for my DSSC entrance exam with rejuvenated vigour and with your blessing should qualify.

4. I must confess that my association with SFF was of a special kind that covered all the facets of life. I shall continue to cherish this memory in times to come. In fact, I am indebted to you for all the help that came so readily

from you all. It would be unfair, as well as, unjustified if I attempt to sum up my association and confine it to this letter. Every aspect of it, will take a letter or so to be able to define it. In spite of my earnest efforts, I failed to measure upto your expectations, which I sincerely realise and despite this a compassionate view by you will ever make me hold you in high esteem. Sir, I give a lot to the org and will ever remain a good ambassador of SFF to Indian Army.

5. Regards to Mrs Uban.

With warm regards,

Sd/

Maj Gen GS Uban, AVSM
Inspector General
SFF, c/o 56 APO

It's unimaginable that Jatin Anand could supply "Simonds" make crampons at a rate lesser than IMF (which charges a price that is free of import duty). Either Jatin Anand got "Simonds" crampons smuggled or he would have supplied duplicate crampons. IG Uban and P/offer Lt Col P. Awasthi knew this fact. Otherwise, how would do they justify this procurement from Jatin's firm Malik Chand and Co and not from IMF. Ideally, crampons should have been bought more in number but since this dealer had only 80 pairs hence whole board proceeding was manipulated to suit him. He got the maximum order courtesy his closeness to the presiding officer which I had brought out in both the confidential letters addressed to Lt Col Pankaj Awasthi.

Same Jatin Anand of Dehradun continues to do good business with the IMA. People like him possess an uncanny knack of getting close to the officers of questionable integrity and in the bargain extract dubious profit by doing unfair business with the Army.

The Last ACR and Goodbye!

All moves were made to shunt me out of the SFF Academy prematurely since I had exposed the bungling made in the purchases of mountaineering equipment.

The board proceedings pertaining to procurement of mountaineering equipment were to be forwarded to HQ SFF by 19 Oct 1999. Since I had refused to be party to this improper purchase by withdrawing my name, the Presiding Officer was busy tightening all loose ends in connivance with Comdt, HQ 22 Est, Brig KN Mehra. Even when they were reminded about the 'long overdue' proceedings, they took almost couple of months to give the procurement a semblance of correct procurement. I persisted with my stance and wrote two confidential letters resultant of which the whole tender process was cancelled. But when the firm STIKAGE threatened to move court against the order cancellation, the equipment was re-ordered.

In the end, I had to pay a price as my ACR was spoilt. But what pains me the most is the manner in which the whole episode was dealt with. Brig KN Mehra lacked guts to endorse my ACR while I was on their posted strength. It was sent to me by post contrary to orders on the subject.

22 Est being an organisation away from the watchful eyes of the Army is left to be run entirely on the whims and fancies of the Commandant 22 Est. The Commandant had an extended run of tenure as he toed the line of IG SFF. In turn he earned his VSM. He was always desperate to undo his previous Bde Cdr tenure at Gwalior and even went to the extent of taking an ad hoc command at the Kargil conflict location. In Army circles his ulterior motive could be seen, hence the move was a no-go.

I was to write ACR of IA pers posted at the SFF Academy. Accordingly, Head Clk prepared ACR forms of all soldiers for me to initiate their ACRs. Lt Col Pankaj Awasthi got apprehensive that I might record some facts related to manipulative purchases of mountaineering equipment in the soldiers' reports. Hence overnight a new set of forms were prepared and another officer Maj Rajneesh Handa was instructed to reinitiate the ACRs. I brought this to the notice of next Cdr SFF but to no avail. It's pity to see a helpless and hapless Commander in your chain of command. The irony is that these incompetent officers are empowered to endorse your confidential report. One doesn't need rocket science to understand whether their reporting will be subjective or objective.

I could have easily moved out of the SFF Academy before 03rd March 2008 as per my posting order and thereby could have avoided the adverse ACR report which led to my supersession. But not well-versed with the tricks of trade, I requested for an extended stay of two weeks without any fear of getting an adverse ACR in the organisation's interest. I wanted to be present at the Admn inspection of the SFF Academy on 16 March 2000. Later on, as expected, my ACR was not endorsed in my presence. In violation of norms, it was forwarded to me by post.

Paradoxically, my attempts to bring corrupt practices by some officers to the notice of higher-ups had sealed my career. I had started taking stand against corruption early in my career without realising that senior Army Officers only pay lip-service while uttering these words – duty, honour, nation's interest. etc.

How come officers personal traits go unnoticed till they attain General officer rank. Army is living with these harsh realities but it seems they have found discreet but surely less effective ways of dealing with them or else how corrupt practices go unnoticed for so long. How do they succeed in hoodwinking the system right from SSB days. I have touched this issue at length in this book. Each officer is reported upon by three seniors, still, their weaknesses surface up only when they attain higher rank.

Recently, an anomaly in the purchase of 150 parachutes from two Ukraine companies was brought to the notice by a Colonel on deputation to this organisation. Refusing to budge from his tough stance he was posted back to Indian Army.

No inquiries! No investigations!!

Quiet burial like my case of the mountaineering equipment purchase.

The latest revelation by Army Chief, Gen VK Singh on 29th March, 2012 regarding rampant corruption in 'procurement scams' in the Special Frontier Forces testifies what I have been harping upon since 1999. I hope the matter will be investigated deeply by the investigating agencies in its entire sincerity.

CHAPTER 5

Power Play

My posting to 2 Sect RR was resultant of my operational performance as Company Commander in the same operational zone, where I broke the backbone of terrorist organisation. All my predecessors in this appointment had an excellent career profile and befittingly rose to higher rank. From May 2003 to Dec 2003 I had the good fortune of serving under Brigadier, KPS Rana who knew my worth and went on to put on record my professional credentials:

"I write to put on record my deep appreciation for your personal contribution in making my task easy as Cdr 2 Sector RR. You worked very hard and provided sound advise on operational matters enabling me to take opt decisions. Your sincere and willing sp made my tenure a memorable one. I thank you for all the co-op and unlimited sp."

In Dec 2003, Brig TS Gill took over as the Commander and developed an instant liking for my professional acumen on account of my operational briefing during Commander Handing/Taking over. With tireless efforts I succeeded in settling down Commander in his operational role. The Commander was appreciative of my commitment to all my responsibilities. Impressed by my unflinching dedication, he wrote to Brigadier Mudolkar at Army HQ advising him to help me out in processing my statutory complaint. The letter read:

"My GSO-2, Maj Arun Kumar Jha from RAJPUT, bearer of this DO letter, will meet you in person. He has represented against his CR of 2000 (Statutory Complaint). His complaint Regd No is S-10224. He is an 'OUTSTANDING' Offr and being graded so by me, when his CR is due in Jun 2004."

When I learnt about Brigadier VK Singh taking over the command of a formation under which I was posted, I wrote to Military Secretary Branch regarding my premature moving out on promotion. It reads:

Maj Arun Kumar HQ 2 Sect RR
GSO 2 (Ops) C/O 56 APO
48368 / AK / 00 19th Feb 2004

Dear Sir,

1. I feel constrained to write to you in this manner, but in the prevailing circumstances, I could think of nothing else than to apprise you regarding the precarious situation I am presently in. I tried to contact you on telephone but I was told by your office that you are presently out of station and will return on 23rd Feb. This being a confidential issue, I decided to pen down relevant facts instead of approaching the officiating Col MS. This letter will give you an insight into my problem and later on by first week of March, I will come over and meet you to

explain in detail my case. On your return next week, I'll also contact you on telephone.

2. In the year 1994, while in 2 Rajput, I had problems with my Commanding Officer, then, Col VK Singh. The seriousness of the issue can be gauged from the fact that I had to approach Allahabad High Court to seek justice[1]. Several observations were made against the Commanding Officer by the court. I will show you the copy of the judgement once I meet you in March.

3. Further, I had also put up a statutory complaint against the CR endorsed by him in Jan. 1994. The complete assessment of his was expunged by MS Br due to its subjectivity.

4. I moved to 23rd Rajput for the glacier tenure and thereafter my panel got changed to 24 Rajput since Oct. 1994.

5. Sir, leaving behind the incident, I started fresh in 24 Rajput. Since then, I have worked hard and am back in the main stream. In nutshell, I attended DSSC, prior to that, voluntarily move to unit for CI tenure and earned a near outstanding report. After staff course, I was once again in CT environment and this time got an Army Cdr's commendation card for a gallant action and also earned an OUTSTANDING ACR. Recently, I have been approved for Lt Col.

6. In all probability, Brig VK Singh, YSM is taking over as GOC CIF (V). Day before he was in this Sector for briefing in the capacity of GOC designate. 2 Sect forms an integral part of victor force. This way, if I complete 30 days under him, I will have to take a CR from him, he being the SRO.

7. You will understand my predicament. I genuinely and truly apprehend that I may not only be harmed in my CR but also directly/indirectly may once again undergo harassment[2].

---

1 **Indifferent MS Branch.** Remained non-committal on my posting but how do they explain my leaving prematurely without relief later on.

2 **Harassment.** I was apprehensive of Gen VK Singh's vindictive thoughts and true to my apprehension he directed Brig TS Gill to sort me out.

8. Sir, these developments have forced me to approach you and seek your pers intervention or if deem fit, timely assistance from MS Branch to view the case in its entirety and post me out as soon as possible.

With warm regards,
Yours sincerely,
Arun Jha

Col Subrato Saha, YSM
Col MS - 2
Military Secretary's Branch
Army HQ, New Delhi

MMS - Mysterious MS Branch

Unique and inexplicable are MS ways. Posting and promotion are the responsibility of the MS Branch. Less one writes about MS Branch better it is! One set of rules for lesser mortals like us and the other for sons and sons-in-law. As expected, MS Branch did not respond to my above letter. But how do they explain my moving out without relief on 3 June 1994. Never before an important staff post like GSO2 (ops) was vacated w/o relief. Lesser mortals throughout their career are subjected to 'organisational interest' to deprive them of any benefits. But on selected few the same shield of 'organizational interest' is used to bestow favours. Army promotions and postings are considered to be fair and transparent, and there is no subjectivity involved. Do we all agree?

On learning that I am seeking premature posting, my Commander assured me total protection from Brigadier VK Singh through the following note:

TO WHOMSOEVER IT MAY CONCERN

This is to certify that IC 48368A Major Arun Kumar Jha is posted under my Command as GSO 2 (Ops). I am fully aware of his past strained relationship with Maj Gen V K Singh, YSM, GOC CIF(V). I will not bow under any pressure and harm him either professionally or personally.

HQ 2 Sector RR
C/O 56 APO

APO
2004

(T S Gill)
(TS Gill)
Brig
Commander
Cdr
HQ 2 Sector RR
HQ 2 Sector RR

I proceeded on leave and on expected lines things were not the same on my return. Each passing day added to my discomfort. "Man Friday" was suddenly made to feel unwanted. No longer I was considered indispensable. I took it in my stride and drew a line that this was my threshold whatever might be the outcome!

I knew a crucial ACR was in the offing. My stat complaint was under consideration. But I was sure that I would not be left helpless for want of one ACR. After giving a hard thought to the issue, I made up my mind to leave w/o relief. My send-off was unceremonious since the evening before in my dining out speech I had mentioned clearly about the Commander's weaknesses.

Unmindful of my career, I kept moving ahead. The news of Brigadier TS Gill moving to Delhi on a make-shift assignment before joining NDC did shake my conscience. I mulled over the thought of placing on record my heartfelt feelings about Brig TS Gill's misdeeds. It were my friends and well-wishers beside my family who prevailed over saying, "If you can't write then who else will write?" The following is my DO to Brig TS Gill:

CONFIDENTIAL

Lt Col Arun Jha

HQ ARTRAC
Trg Branch
Shimla

AKJ / Pers / 48368

06th June 2005

Dear Brigadier,

1. I received no reply to my letter which I had sent across through a jawan of HQ 2 Sectt RR by hand before boarding the train from Jammu on 06th June '04. I wrote the note with a heavy heart.

2. Once again, I am writing to you to apprise you about your misconduct. I remained quiet for a year just for one reason, that any action of mine should not indirectly affect 2 Sector's performance. I, for one had contributed a lot towards its operational achievements in order to bring it to No. 1 position in the year 2003 in the entire Northern Command. Now, since you are on your way out and will be in unwinding mode, I am penning down once again my feelings. It is done with an aim to make you carry out introspection and maybe, therefore, no one else faces the brunt of your vices.

3. On my return from leave on 06th April 2004, to my surprise, I had found out that nearly one and half lakhs of rupees had been siphoned off within few days. Maj d'Cunha, Offg GSO2 gave me an unconvincing account of the expenditure in his own handwriting (Ref. Appx A).

4. The worst account one could give off is that manipulating something of a dead body. You did this shamelessly. A handwritten chit in Urdu was placed on the slain terrorist's body[3], bearing a Chandigarh residential address. This note was written by none other than a retired soldier of JAK RIF battalion who was employed by the Sector. His name is Mr Bhatt. Supposedly, this was carried out to sort out somebody in Chandigarh who had a tiff/dispute with your brother-in-law. 2 Sect RR forwarded the letter to HQ Victor force (Ref Appx B) and, in turn, it was

3 **Shameless Act!** Worst account a human being can give of herself/himself.

forwarded to BGS (ops), Western Command under letter ref 1031/2 Sect/Docu/GS/dated 21st March 2004.

5. When I learnt about all this and much more that how an office has been misused/abused I immediately within a couple of days applied for balance of leave and furlough till 18th June (Ref. Appx C) a day prior to my relief's reporting on duty. I was persuaded to withdraw my leave application on pretext of organisational interests. Thereafter, you went ahead and gave me a certificate to shelter me against Maj Gen VK Singh on 20th April 2004, with whom I had strained relationship. In any case, I did not require any assurance as I had written to MS Branch regarding my posting on 19th Feb 2004 itself. I would like to mention that had it not been for Maj Gen VK Singh as the GOC and Corps Cdr being your regimental officer, I would have set the record straight.

6. Later on, I also learnt that you had manipulated a sum of Rs. 86,500/- of IT grant and once again it was Maj d'Cunha who did the cover-up action with Board of Officers to legalise the procurement by showing items of ATG in IT list (Ref. Appx D).

7. Your weakness for liquor[4] is known to one and all and that is why you are nicknamed "Tanker". But, we under your command had to bear out your absurd behaviour in your inebriated state. My wife and grown-up daughter, who had joined me only on 16th May 2004, had to request me to pack and leave early after seeing your behaviour in a drunken state especially with the ladies in the Officers Mess. Therefore, I had to cancel my reservations for 24th June 2004 and had to leave abruptly on 05th June without reservation (managed one berth at the last moment). Not only did it cause inconvenience to us but also I had to leave an operational area without a relief. My relief was to report on 19th June 2004 and a proper handing/taking over was to take place. I am sure, now in retrospect, you would appreciate my moral courage and strong convictions[5], especially, when I stood up against you, when my ACR was due on 01st June 2004.

4 Borne the **Brunt of Weakness**.

5 **Self-esteem** irrespective of the crucial ACR, I moved out, as my self-esteem was at stake rather than career progression.

S. No.	Amount	EXPDR	Running Bal	Remarks
1	35,000/-	Deepak	3,85,000/-	
2	40,000/-	Col Paliwal	3,45,000/-	
3	20,000/-	Dy Comdt	3,25,000/-	
4	20,000/-	2 Para	3,05,000/-	
5	20,000/-	1 Para	2,85,000/-	
6	20,000/-	Source 1130	2,65,000/-	
7	10,000/-	Sub Source BHU	2,55,000/-	
8	15,000/-	Prithvi	2,40,000/-	
9	45,000/-	Prithvi	1,95,000/-	
10	10,000/-	ACG (to be returned) Porter Lay	1,85,000/-	
	2,35,000/-			

Appx A

GE Dec	2,20,000/-
GOC	1,00,000/-
2×50,000/-	1,00,000/-
	4,20,000/-
+	10,000/-
	4,30,000/-
To give	5,000/-
	4,35,000/-

Abdulla to give Rs 15,000/-
given 10,000/-

5,000/-

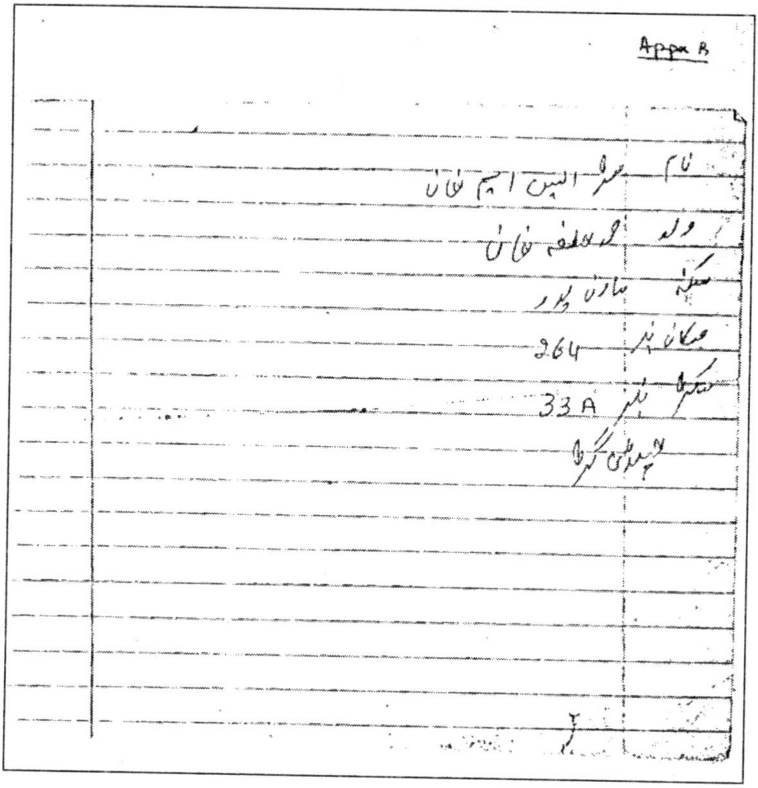
Appx B

نام

ولد

سکنہ

مکان نمبر 264

سیکٹر نمبر 33 A

Appx C

आई०ए०एफ०लि०-118
I.A.F.L.-1184

अफसरों के लिए छुट्टी का आवेदन पत्र
OFFICER'S APPLICATION FOR LEAVE

1. सं०, रैंक और नाम
No., Rank and Name....IC 48368 A MAJ ARUN KUMAR JHA

2. यूनिट
Unit ....HQ 2 Sect RR..............

3. नियुक्ति
Appointment ....GSO 2 (OPS)..............

4. ड्यूटी के लिए प्रबंध
Arrangement for performance of duty.....Sect Mng..........

5. अब अफसरों की सं०
No. of Officers remaining..........07..........

6. वार्षिक/फर्लो/बीमारी/आकस्मिक छुट्टी जिसके लिए आवेदन दिया गया है
.... से .... तक के लिए (दिनों की संख्या)
Annual/furlough/~~sick/casual~~ leave applied from....10 Apr 04........
to....18 June 04....................(No. of days 67
BAL - 27 days and furlough for 40 days wef 09 May 04.

7. छुट्टी के दौरान का पता
Address on leave........F 211, RAJ TI MARG, SHAHJAHANPUR 233833 (UP)

8. कितने दिन की आकस्मिक छुट्टी ली
Days casual leave applied..........Nil..........

9. स्थान तारीख आवेदक के हस्ताक्षर
Station....95 SO APO....Date....08 Apr 04....Signature of applicant

Appx D   D4 CDR & P' Spk

IT GRANT

1. Total amount Alloted - 325000/-
2. Supply Order placed - 325000/-
3. Items being procured out of IT Grant

ITEMS DEMANDED WITH COST

S No	Items	Qty	Rate	Total amount
1.	PCs	06	35000 /-	2,10000/-
2.	UPS	06	6000 /-	36000/-
3.	DMP	04	15000 /-	60,000/-
4.	CD Writer	03	1x 6000= 6000 /- 2x 6500= 13000/-	19000/-
			Total Rs	3,25000/-

(Total amount three lac twenty thousand only)

ATG

1. Amount Debit as on 25 May - 110087/- — Next allotment
2. Items procured since 25 May Till now of Amt - 3,44408/- — Jul 04, Sep 04 & Jan 04
3. Total payment due - 4,24496/-
4. Amt sanction (ATG + IT Sty) - 3,25000/-

Debit to Prepaid - 9,9496/- | 04 CDR to spk pl.

ITEMS ALREADY PROCURED OUT OF ATG AND TO BE TAKEN ON CHARGE OF IT ITEMS

S No	Items	Qty	Rate	Total
1.	PC - IV	01	35,000/-	35,000/-
2.	PC - III	02	15,000/-	30000/-
3.	DMP	01	15,000/-	15,000/-
4.	CD Writer	01	6500/-	6500/-
			Total Rs	86,500/-

Grp shown

(Total amount Rs eighty six thousand five thousand only)

8. Also, your parochial attitude was at its limit, as all the Sikh officers were rated outstanding in the ACR. Even, an officer who had married a Sikh lady was the beneficiary.

9. The uprightness on my part costed me dearly. It was reliably learnt, that on my departure, you had approached Col AK Mudholkar in the complaint Advisory Board of Army HQ. Col Mudholkar was posted with you at Army War College, Mhow in the same faculty just a few months back. As a result, my statutory complaint got a subjective look. I am of the opinion that this is the main reason for my statutory complaint getting rejected or else why I would have not got even partial redressal when others with a question mark on professional integrity got substantial redressal during the same period. As you are aware, my ACR in consideration for redressal was entirely based on a non-professional issue i.e. family discord.

10. It would take a lifetime and pages after pages to bring out your misdemeanour[6]. The other striking one is that right throughout many terrorist group intercepts raised enough doubts about the authenticity of killings of terrorists. A case in point was the killing which took place in 36 RR area of Resp by 5 Para on 15th/16th May night.

11. People like you have damaged the moral fibre of this organisation to a large extent. My only request to you now is that never ever we come across each other. I would request that even if such a situation arises you being a senior officer, kindly ensure it is avoided.

Yours Sincerely
Arun Jha

Brig TS Gill, VSM
Cdr
HQ 2 Sect RR
C/O 56 APO

---

6 **Misdemeanour.** Inexplicable misconduct for career enhancement.

Power Corrupts

You are within your rights to carry out any legitimate actions for furtherance of your career. An inadvertent action to boost your career can also be acceptable as long as it is in the national interest. But how do you justify inhuman and indecent conduct for moving up the ladder in the Army hierarchy?

Brig TS Gill carried on recklessly his action without any repentance as he enjoyed the patronage of his superiors, Gen VK Singh being his immediate boss. His entire focus was to sort me out and he made a sincere attempt at that. Thanks to his remarkable ability to follow his superior's diktat in letter and spirit, today he has risen to almost top of the ladder. His professional calibre is certainly not up to the mark. If one is vested with power and authority, it means more the power, more the accountability. But what I witnessed was just contrary - lot of power and no accountability at all. Power corrupts and absolute power corrupts absolutely.

Despotic Style of Functioning

Brig TS Gill's despotic style of functioning was attributable to two main factors. Firstly, he enjoyed the patronage of Maj Gen VK Singh and secondly his reviewing officer (for ACR) was from his own regiment. A convincing proof of bestowing favours surreptitiously on Brig Gill was the realignment of the Sector boundary just before his taking over of the Command of 2 Sect RR. It was done to help him remain ahead in the number game (body counts!). When due to harassment by Brig Gill I left the Sector prematurely, he was awarded an "outstanding" ACR. Thereafter, he moved to Delhi with high chances of his attending NDC at New Delhi. But, his posting as Brig Adm of the Corps under Lt Gen VK Singh away from Delhi surprised many officers. However, it did not come as a surprise to me because I knew Brig Gill was awarded for his loyalty by Lt Gen VK Singh.

A leading English daily of Bhuvneshwar highlighted the objection raised by MOD over Major General TS Gill's name approved for staff appointment in the next rank. After realizing that Maj General TS Gill cannot qualify for 'command' category due to his age, his name was approved for 'Staff only' category despite his low marks. The MOD objection has resulted in delay of various projects as at many critical posts officiating incumbents are holding the post and they are not vested with financial authority. Further, this delay has created an atmosphere of uncertainty as many officers are not sure of picking up the next rank before due date of their retirement.

I leave it to the readers to judge whether a man of TS Gill demeanour deserves the rank of Lt General!

Kashmir – Victim of Circumstances

Kashmir is blessed with abundant natural beauty justifying its description as 'Paradise on Earth'. But look at the curse this paradise has to live with. The British divide and rule policy affected this state the most. If three Indo-Pak wars were not enough to cause agonising pain to the Kashmiri people, the rise of terrorism has forced them to live in war-like situation over the last two decades. But, ironically, it seems everyone is thriving in this situation. That's why efforts to bring normalcy in Kashmir have come to naught time and again. Common people understand the problem of Kashmir through the distorted lens of the mainstream national media.

I feel majority of the locals are not interested in furthering the agenda of the terrorists. All they want is peaceful living and prosperity. Not long ago, they were known for their simple approach to life and peaceful Hindu-Muslim co-existence. But some elements, abetted by the destabilising forces across the border, have been exploiting the State's demographic patterns and religious affinities to widen the wedge between Kashmiri Hindus and Muslims thus giving a moral boost to the terrorists.

To wean the Kashmiri youth away from the influence of separatist leaders and terrorists, tourism development is the best bet. Singapore will be forgotten as a holiday destination as it stands nowhere near the nature's beautiful bounties bestowed on Pahalgam, Gulmarg, Ladakh, Srinagar and other exotic locales of the State. Infrastructure development alongside Dal Lake will give tourists a mesmerising holiday apart from providing the Valley's disillusioned youth much needed employment for peaceful, normal living. These disillusioned youth will come back to the mainstream and will no longer indulge in stone pelting acts or joining the ranks of terrorists.

Today due to numerous avoidable as well unavoidable actions on the part of security forces, the energy of these youths is getting channelized in a negative way. One example of this is the rage and fury that erupts among these youths against the search operations conducted by security forces in their houses. Doesn't this rage manifest in the shape of terror attacks in metropolitan cities? Weren't the threads of the September 2011 bomb blast at the Delhi High Court linked to this rage?

Despite the Army's *sadbhavna* projects, few Army operations have drawn sharp criticism from the locals. The Security Forces are unable to mollify the youth rage. That's why the militant organisations across the border succeed in exploiting these disillusioned youth for implementing their sinister plans in the Valley and elsewhere in India. Hence, the need of the hour is to handle the delicate and sensitive issue of Kashmir with maturity and not leaving any scope for discontentment among the local people. We have better track record of Human Rights viz US, China and Pakistan. To do this honestly, a key factor is the accountability of the powers that be in the civilian and Army setups. However, accountability seems to be the least concern of these very authorities.

Ignorance is Bliss!

Maj Gen VK Singh and Corps Cdr of Brig TS Gill cannot shirk their responsibility by stating that they did not know what was going on and what was the intent behind Brig TS Gill's misdemeanour. With some CI experience one can easily judge that all the unscrupulous actions on the part of Brig TS Gill were for furtherance of his career.

Failure Rewarded!

The worst IED attack in JandK history was witnessed on 26 May 2004, approximately two and half km away from HQ 2 Sect RR. The down convoy bus carrying passengers (including ladies and children) were charred to death. For this attack, the CRPF was blamed, citing dereliction of duty by its personnel as ROP (Road Opening Party) was their responsibility. But Cdr 2 Sector RR was awarded an outstanding ACR in a month after the attack by Maj Gen VK Singh for operational performance.

Here an obvious poser is: Area dominance was whose responsibility? Had 2 Sector RR carried out its task and operational role in a befitting manner then the IED attack could have been prevented. But here we saw the gross neglect of accountability in not assessing the failure of 2 Sector RR in preventing this attack. Ignoring this failure, the performance of Cdr 2 Sector RR was graded outstanding just because in his tenure as Commander he had managed to add impressive number of kills.

Misconduct on the part of Brig TS Gill displayed a series of behavioural aberrations as far as the Army ethos is concerned. This was nothing but highly selfish concern for the advancement of an officer's career. This degradation of military values had its cascading effect on officers posted under his command. All actions carried out for personal advancement was in stark contrast to the Chetwode saying.

All those occupying powerful posts must understand that "no power is absolute." For the misuse of power, sooner or later they themselves or the nation will have to pay a heavy price. It is understandable, that an officer is required to build a career but he should first build a better India. This country deserves the best from a soldier.

Chapter 6

Alma Mater

After a successful stint at ARTRAC (Army Training Command) I received the order for my posting to Dehradun. As usual, routine activities prior to moving out from a military station were carried out in the nick of time. However, a dampener on my excitement came in the form of verbal orders from the Army HQ MS Br that my posting had been held in abeyance.

I was feeling helpless and frustrated, as I had already been relieved from my appointment and was raring to move to next assignment. Lt Col Kamal Dev, GSO (Coord) Training Br, wrote to MS Br that the officer had obtained TC (Transfer Certificate) from school, got gas cylinder deposited, etc. etc. and was all set to move with his house in a completely packed state, hence his move should not be stalled. In response, my posting was diverted to the IMA (Indian Military Academy) in Dehradun itself.

Tenure at IMA

It's a dream come true for an officer to be posted at his Alma Mater. My new assignment was demanding and absorbing. In right earnest I carried out all the tasks that were assigned to me. I passed my mandatory physical tests and was declared fit to be retained at the IMA.

I undertook my posting at the Alma Mater with a pledge to pay back in whatever little way I could. Although, I was superseded but my zeal and vigour made it easy for me to make my presence felt, I got out-of-turn allotment for accommodation since my stay inside the IMA premises was a necessity for smooth administrative functioning.

The IMA being a premier training institute, funds amounting to crores of rupees are sanctioned for running it. I saw requisite paper work being meticulously carried out for all purchases made. But one day when I was approached to sign as a member of board of officers regarding stationery purchases by the Comdt's Secretariat, my eyes popped out seeing the figures of stationery. I refused to sign. However, my refusal did not have any impact as things remained the same as earlier. Only my name was replaced by some other officer's name and it was business as usual. But, for me life was not the same thereafter. Senior officers started harassing me on trivial issues.

Since I was battle-hardened, I took the harassment in my stride but it started telling on my health. My BP shot up to 154/106 on 11 Nov 2006. I took up meditation to firm up my resolve.

A cursory glance at the highly abnormal consumption of stationery (some items) by Commandant's secretariat in one quarter will give the reader an idea how deep was the rot? Details of some of the stationery consumption (approximate quantities) by Comdt's Secretariat in one quarter are as under:

Articles	A/U	Qty
Executive Bond Paper	Ream	215
Typing Paper	Ream	887
Pen Add Gel	Nos	432
Carbon Cases	Pkt	518
Photo Stat Paper	Ream	407
Photo Stat Paper A-3	Ream	238
Duplicating Paper	Ream	603

How can anyone justify this huge stationery consumption by the Comdt's Secretariat! The Comdt of a premier institute is a posting of high integrity. It's unfortunate that the General officer took no interest in enhancing the training standards of the Military Academy but took this posting as his resettlement opportunity. Sad! That's the main reason why cadets' accommodation and the mess project got inordinately delayed.

Things came to a head when I had to reply to a demeaning confidential letter. My reply is reproduced as under:

CONFIDENTIAL

Indian Military Academy
Dehradun

48368/AJ 01 November 2006

Brig. Ashok Pillai [1]
BGS
GS Branch,
IMA

Dear Sir,

1. Ref letter No. 27632/Confd/Offrs dt. 31 Oct, 2006.

1 Same BGS was later summoned for purchases made out of ATG for microlight aircraft.

2. I had got my return railway reservation by Train No. 3009 Dehradun Express from Lucknow to Dehradun on 29 Oct 2006. The train was scheduled to arrive at Dehradun at 0645 hrs on 31st Oct 2006. Due to derailment en route, the train was late by eleven hrs and it reached Dehradun Rly Stn at 1745 hrs.

3. It is submitted that I continuously updated Maj Gaurav Shukla, Offg GSO-1 (Coord) regarding the late running of train.

4. I assure you that in future I will be extra cautious in terms of keeping cushion while travelling by train during leave.

(**Arun Jha**)

Lt Col

GSO - 1 (Coord)

Seniors continued to trouble me. The following letter from IO provides an insight into their malafide intentions:

CONFIDENTIAL

Tele: 0135-2705211 GS Branch

Indian Military Academy
Dehradun - 248007
37355/RS
03 November 2006

Lt Col AK Jha
GSO - 1 (Coord)
GS Branch, IMA

COUNSELLING

1. I have noted with great concern that you are not discharging your duties as GSO-1 (Coord) of GS Branch efficiently. You are lacking sincerety of purpose, hardwork and dedication. You often do not complete the task assigned to you within the given time frame which causes unnecessary delay and avoidable embarrassment. To cite just one such of lapse is that you were given the task of obtaining input on achievements of IMA in last one year from various brochures and put up draft on

the next day which was not completed even after 3 days. You had not carried out your duties satisfactorily in my absence which was conveyed to me by the BGS in your presence on 01 November and for which I issued a verbal warning to you to show distinct change in your working attitude and functioning. You have totally disregarded this advice and continued with your callous and negative attitude to the extent that you have of late started defying orders. It is evident from the facts that you did not put up absence brief to me on my return from lve and T/D on your own which is not as per the existing norms on 01 Nov 06 . You were asked to put up the same by the end of office hours which you failed to do so even by end of the third working day i.e. 03 Nov. 06.

2. You have been counselled on numerous occasions earlier but to no avail. You are hereby advised once again to take interest and perform your duties efficiently with diligence and dedication to the org failing which I will be forced against my wishes to initiate necessary action against you.

(Ranbir Singh)
Col
Col GS

CONFIDENTIAL

Everyone started exploiting the uncertainty of my stay at the IMA by issuing inconsequential warnings. My reply to the above counselling letter of Col Ranbir Singh is reproduced below:

COUNSELLING

1. Refer your letter No. 37355/RS dated 03 November 2006.
2. At the outset, I tender my apology for resorting to this means of comn. Your statement in the letter under ref that I am not discharging my duties efficiently is incorrect. To sp my statement, I wish to draw your kind attn to some

of the tasks which I have carried out effectively without guidance:

a) Heptr Demand for Ex Golabari: Draft letter/applications were recd from trg team on 29 Sept 2006. These were returned back to trg team on 06 Oct 2006 with minor obsns. Keeping the delay in mind on one account or the other, I had to perforce sign and fwd it to HQ West Com and HQ ARTRAC on 11 Oct 2006 for materialization of demand by 15 Oct 2006.

b) Fwd of Letters to Fmn Outside IMA: I have personally fwd more than 50% letters/sign to higher HQs and even the letters which have been fwd under your signatures have been mainly drafted by me.

c) Prep of Minutes of Weekly Confs: Within 24 hrs, draft of mins of weekly confs are prep and put up on minute sheet.

d) Presentation on Choice of Arms: Within a short notice of 2 hrs, I took a presentation on Choice of Arms at Khetarpal Auditorium on 09 Sep 2006. It is pertinent to mention that I was posted to IMA just about 1½ months back.

e) Shouldering Addl Responsibilities: Within less than a month of service in the Academy, I performed the duties of GSO-2 (Stats). The task involved compiling the periodic assessment of character qualities.

f) Briefing and Presentation to Foreign Academies: I was detailed to give a briefing to Australian Def Forces Academy and RMC Duntroon, Australia, during their visit to IMA.

g) Prep of Mementoes: On many occasions, I have got the mementoes prep on directions of Comdt at a very-very short notice.

h) Distr of Sweets on Diwali: On this day at 0930 hrs, I recd the instrs to distribute sweets to nearly thirty people incl VVIPs. I coord this task to the entire satisfaction of BGS.

i) Assistance to PRO: All the press releases of PRO are drafted by me since Capt Sonia Khatri has been made incharge of PRO Cell.

j) Activities related to POP: Right from issuing of gen instrs to coord of events at Rashtrapati Bhawan, has been carried out by me. Gen instrs were reqd to be issued by 30 Sep 2006, which I had to finally issue a day after you proceeded on leave i.e. on 19 Oct 06. Further, the correspondence to MT-6 was also fwd by me which actually should have been fwd by 15 Oct 06.

k) Selfless Commitment: I have never attended Parents Teachers Meet at my daughter's school. Also, I have never accompanied my wife and children to MH. Never before 1500 hrs, I have left the office and I also coord many activities from my residence.

3. It's really unfortunate that I have to justify my commitment and dedication. On many occasions, I have personally got the office re-opened at odd hours and have executed the assigned task. The load of my work can be gauged from the No. of letters I take out in a day and similarly No. of calls I receive/make per day.

4. Heptr Demand for Ex Chakravyuh: Trg Team had fwd draft letter/applications for placing heptr demand for Ex Chakravyuh on 11 Oct 2006. Ideally, within a day or two, it should have been fwd to HQ West Com and HQ ARTRAC under your signatures or at least before you proceeded on leave on 18 Oct 2006. Nevertheless, I took the complete blame on myself without putting fwd any excuse when heptr demand was not fwd in time. You would appreciate that the slip-up was mainly because the concerned subject was dealt by a GC Orderly (performing the duties of clerk) in absence of permanent clerk.

5. Absence Brief: I would like to humbly submit that never before an absence brief has been put up to Col GS. Even, on your return from PAL on 18 August 2006, no absence brief was put up. However, OS was asked to put up all the correspondence duly flagged for your info on 01 November 2006. On the contrary, I would like to kindly bring to your notice that no handing/taking over pts were given by you before you proceeded on leave on

18 Oct 06. The slip-up on account of heptr demand for Ex Chakravyuh would have probably not happened if handing/taking over pts would have been made. Even when I proceeded on three days C/L, I handed over pending pts in writing to Maj Gaurav Shukla.

6. Performance: 01 Nov to 03 Nov 06: To be specific, I drafted DO letter for Lt Gen Surinder Nath on 01 Nov, put up a draft DO letter for JAT Regt Silver Medal on 02 Nov and on 03 Nov, I have put up a draft letter regarding IMA i.e. reqd to be sent across to President Sectt.

7. Draft DO letter for COAS: If you recall, I had put up Annual Trg Report and few correspondence on achievements of IMA on 14 Oct 2006 for your analysis and proper vetting. Finally, on 16 Oct 2006, I took few clarifications from the BGS regarding the content of the letter and drafted the DO. There was no reqmt to incl the results of 30km speed march or any other specific input, but all that was reqd was to highlight all major activities with broad results in the last one year.

8. Your statement at Para 2 of letter quoted under ref, wherein you have stated that you have been counselled on numerous occasions is misleading. You have made generic remarks regarding functioning of GS Branch in morning conf. on few occasions but never in specific you have verbally counselled me.

9. Sir, you would agree upon that in spite of putting up best of efforts there is a likelihood of some error. Even, the counselling letter under ref has spelling and grammatical mistakes.

Till date, I have never been counselled for my professional work. I promise you about my dedication and commitment. In future, I will be extra cautious while handling dak. My endeavour will be not to provide you with an opportunity to counsel me, but I would also like to earnestly request you to refrain from foul mouthing.

(Arun Jha)
Lt Col
GSO-2 (Coord)

CONFIDENTIAL

Note: In ACR such letter references are endorsed in the Column of Warning and thereafter one gets involved in a vicious circle of stat and non-stat complaints. Lucky enough if one gets redressal, otherwise one is written off for life. For someone when redressal is seen as glass half empty they dig out everything from SSB days but for intent of granting redressal to selective few they see glass half filled. That's the reason in case of Gen VK Singh his past records were not tallied.

What was My Fault?

Why should I have become party to a fraudulent purchase, wherein in the name of stationery purchases personal benefits were accruing to senior officers. Fortunately for me the new Comdt took charge and things settled down nicely. I brought to his notice that I almost became a victim of circumstances and was about to be posted out. The new Comdt in the fitness of things prematurely posted out Col Ranbir Singh, who was instrumental in harassing me at the behest of former Commandant. Gradually, IMA realized how the previous Comdt had manipulated the whole system for his personal gains.

When things were solely under my control I tried my best to take care of the IMA interest. As against exorbitant rates at which purchases were made at the IMA, I bought books for GCs at nearly 30% discount during platinum jubilee celebrations. As ever, I drew strength from my principled stand against corruption. It is pertinent to mention here that on my insistence probably for the first time in the history of IMA a sum of Rs. 10 lakhs was surrendered in February 2008 from ATG (Annual Training Grant).

Devious way to hide Aircraft Destruction

During my IMA tenure, I saw another facet of General officers' misdemeanour. The Comdt took a liking for a micro light aircraft that was meant for GCs training. He enjoyed overseeing IMA training by taking a bird's-eye view while flying the micro light aircraft. No hassle in pursuing this hobby as IMA resources were at his disposal! Using these resources in whichever way was his prerogative! He logged several hours of flying which almost earned him a place in the Limca Book of World Records. But one fine day the micro light aircraft which he was flying was almost destroyed in an accident while landing. Then a whopping Rs 18 lakhs were shown to be incurred on the aircraft repairs. Actually, the parts were shown to be bought in a way so as to keep the purchases within the spending powers of the Comdt, that is Rs 60,000. This way a new micro light aircraft came into being while in records all expenses were shown to be spent on the repairs of the old micro light aircraft. Up the chain all capable and competent officers conveniently moved the minute sheet in bargain for their petty gains.

This fact surfaced when there was a major fire accident in which parts of the micro light aircraft got burnt in the store. A court of inquiry was ordered to assess and regularise the damage. But to everyone's surprise it was discovered that the aviation stores which got burnt were not held on charge of the training team. This opened a can of worms.

To get to the truth, GS Branch sent across the vouchers for renewal of all stores that were purchased from the ATG fund the previous year. The stores which got burnt were not taken on charge, hence there was a mismatch between GS Branch purchase and stores held with the training team. A court of inquiry was ordered to investigate the matter. Previous BGS IMA was called upon but he refused to answer the questions of the Presiding Officer of the Court as the latter was a junior officer. After much dilly-dallying a staff court of inquiry was ordered from the Central Command to look into the matter. Following this inquiry, it was discovered that the micro light aircraft stores worth 18 lakhs were purchased by breaking up the purchases. But instead of stores worth 18 lakhs a new micro light aircraft came into wing whose actual cost was Rs 14 lakhs. This test audit report brought out this glaring irregularity that was beyond any one's comprehension.

Costly Chetwode Clock Repairs

When a cadet joins the IMA, he sets his foot in the cradle of learning leadership qualities. In a short span of time, he transforms himself from man to leader. At 'Antim Pag' he is filled with enthusiasm to lead his men in most challenging situations. The Chetwode clock remains embedded in the memory of alumnus of the IMA forever. Besides being a pleasing site, it instils a sense of discipline in all cadets as they stick to their rigorous routine.

During my tenure, the Chetwode clock required frequent repairs. In two such repairs a stupendous amount of Rs 11 lakhs were spent. The costly repairs of Chetwode clock and the micro light aircraft stores purchase left little money to run the IMA. This reality was brought to the notice of the Central Army Commander by the new IMA Commandant.

Scapegoat

True to the Indian Army tradition, a scapegoat was found to cover up the financial irregularity at IMA. The Col Adm of IMA who was to move on promotion as Brigadier in a couple of days was given 'Drop in performance'. We were helpless witness to this sad episode. I would have also met the same fate had I not put up a stiff resistance. Unfortunately, in the Army today tough stance is misconstrued as fighting the system. Nobody is ready to hold your hand and you become a social outcast. By now, I had developed a habit of living with it, so I lived happily with it and performed my duties.

Delayed PMR

I had applied for pre-mature retirement (PMR) on 1 May 2008 to be relieved by 17 Dec 2008, exactly on completion of 20 years of my service. Hence the Comdt took up my case and recommended 6-month extension for me stating that the officer has conducted PM and President POP and is required for RM POP in Dec 2008. But, MS Br in its own inimitable ways posted me out wherein Lt Col KDS Rai who was holding the appointment of Estate Officer was given an extension for six months.

CHAPTER 7

General Salute

A salutation is a mode of greeting or reverential address by word or gesture when two or more persons meet, whether these persons have equal status or are bound by a superior-subordinate relationship. A military salute is an essential form of discipline regulated and enforced by military law. All officers salute on meeting and on making or receiving official reports. Military courtesy requires the junior officer to salute first.

General officers receive salute with much fanfare. A special tune is played when the complete contingent comes to savdhan and salutes General officers. On special occasions they receive salute with the sword. General officers are looked up with awe and respect even on the civvie street courtesy the ranks they wear. A Gentleman Cadet during his training at the Indian Military Academy (IMA) gets inspired by the lectures delivered by General officers on many occasions. And then right from the day of his commissioning at the Passing-out Parade, the Gentleman Cadet hopes and strives to reach/attain this rank.

Sukhna et al a Big Blow to the Prestige of General officers

The rank of a General officer makes anyone sit up and take notice of, hence the conduct of a General officer has to be above board all the time. But in the recent past, some General officers have been found wanting in the conduct behoving their status. Despite the Army's massive internal clean-up ordered in the wake of the Tehelka expose in 2001, at least 20 officers of the rank of Brigadier and above have been indicted in various corruption-related cases. In the past few years, at least 10 officers of the rank of General were indicted in various cases of corruption and moral turpitude. Major General AK Lal was dismissed when found guilty of molesting a lady officer. In February 2012, a retired Vice Chief of Army was also in news for land related issues at Pune, where he was Army Commander.

Among the glaring corruption cases involving Army officers, the Sukhna land scam figures prominently. What makes the Sukhna scam so special is the fact that an entire chain of command was involved in giving the builder an NOC. Hence the entire chain of command – beginning from the GOC of 33 Corps, his Chief of Staff, the Brigadier (administration) to the Delhi-based Military Secretary – has been indicted for their alleged role.

The findings of the court of inquiry (COI) which went into the Sukhna land deal are yet to become fully known, but it is clear that the Army will study its implications for long. For instance, what will be the impact of the Sukhna indictment on the office of the Military Secretary (MS), one of the eight principal Staff Officers who report to the Army Chief and are handpicked by him. The MS not only heads all the promotion boards of the Army but also handles the postings of all officers above the rank of Colonel. He also hands out the gallantry awards and foreign postings of officers. According to a retired officer, "It will take the Army years to erase the perceived taint on the office of the Military Secretary."

Army analysts warn that the Sukhna scam will lead to an increasingly cautious Army. Senior officers will become wary of dealing with anything connected with land or with large procurements. It will lead to a nervous chain of command that will think twice before implementing orders received from their superiors. All these spell serious repercussions for an Army that demands unquestioned compliance of orders.

My Course Grading not Justified

Junior Command Course (JC) is considered to be an important career course. Like any other officer I went prepared and remained focused to do well as I was always confident of performing well. I fared above average by scoring good marks. Returned happily and content to join SFF Academy as an Instructor. However, I was taken aback to receive course grading which read "B". It's not the grading which affected me but the manner in which it was awarded. The course grading is displayed on the termination of the course to lend credibility to the whole process. Here it was not the case. At once, I brought this to the notice of the Commander JC Wing in writing. The following reply of the Commander JC Wing shows the high-headedness of General Officer, reflecting colonial legacy:

CONFIDENTIAL

Junior Command Wing
College of Combat
Mhow (M.P.) 453441

4703 / ASI / JC 27th JUNE 1998

The Commandant
Special Frontier Force Academy
HQ Establishement No. 22
C/o 56 APO

JC GRADING : MAJ ARUN KUMAR

1. Photo copy of Letter No. 48368/AK/Pers dated 28th May 98 addressed by Maj Arun Kumar is enclosed.
2. The case of officer has been personally scrutinized by the undersigned. There is no substance in any of the arguments put forth by the officer. Maj Arun Kumar failed to get 'instr' grading because he did not have the requisite number of 'Instr' recommendations from his Directing Staff or the Senior Instructor.
3. It may be seen from the letter that the language used by the officer is down right offensive and unofficer like. He has insinuated manipulation and favouritism by stating following falsehoods:
   - "I have come to know from other colleagues that even with 57% marks some have secured "B" grading and Offrs who have just managed 61%/62% marks in written have been awarded B (I)".
   - "The Offrs with 67%/68% have been pulled up to A (I) grading".
4. Maj Arun Kumar may please be asked to name the Offrs who have allegedly been awarded "B" grading with 57% marks and "A" with 67 to 68%. The particulars so obtained may please be forwarded to this Headquarters.
5. It is requested that following instrs be issued to all the officers detailed to JC Course in future:

- o Not to address any letter directly to the College of Combat (Comdt/Cdr) on matters pertaining to course gradings.
- o Desist from making false statements/allegations against the organisation.

We consider the case is closed as far as this wing is concerned. However we request you to forward the name of officers as requested vide para 4 above, which may be obtained from Maj Arun Kumar.

(VS Karnik)
Maj Gen
Cdr

Copy to :-
Maj Arun Kumar
Special Frontier Force Academy

How Silly?

I had the courage of conviction to write about the grading system. Probably first time in General Saheb life someone would have written to him in such a befitting manner. He was immature enough to reply back promptly to Commandant HQ 22 Est. I found the reply amusing as he stated that case is closed from their end but wanted me to forward names of the officers. A responsible officer would have stated that the names be forwarded so as to look into the matter.

Instead of taking corrective measures or carrying out introspection after receiving my hard-hitting letter, a reply was given immediately to the Comdt enclosing my letter. Understandable! As this is the Army way to put an outspoken officer on defensive. But, Maj Gen Saheb in the fitness of things should have taken down the names from me and would have come out with specific rebuttal instead of giving a vague reply. It really sounded silly to state that the case was closed from his end. Once in a while someone writes about some manipulative action, but the General officer instead of taking steps to curb the malaise skirts the issue. Then one feels disappointed by the conduct of the General officer. But gradually one learns to reconcile with such ungraceful conduct on part of the General officer.

In the recent past, General officers have given a sorry account of themselves. A retired Vice Army Chief conduct has also come under cloud. The sanctity of the Army Chief's office has also been vitiated, courtesy the age row of Gen VK Singh.

Gen VK Singh – A Third-Generation Officer!!

A third-generation officer like Gen VK Singh, carrying the legacy of his forefathers, is expected to be more wary of Army ethos and culture. He is supposed to be well versed with the traditions of the Indian Army. However, the account of professionalism and personal conduct of Gen VK Singh in the Army, which is well supported by documentary evidence, tells an altogether different story.

No regimentation, career progression at all costs, placing self before everything, etc, etc. - Does it behove the stature of an Army officer leave aside that of a third generation officer? Here the term third generation could be misleading. Gen VK Singh being a third generation officer should have contributed immensely towards the welfare of the troops. To say the least, an AC train ferrying the jawans on a daily basis from Jammu to New Delhi should have been operated.

Gen VK Singh also missed the opportunity to make valuable contribution in addressing many an important issues besetting the Army. Though like his predecessors, he too made a beginning with a loud bang but very soon he got embroiled in his own issues. The Chief of the Army Staff, who is a repository of the faith of a million plus men in uniform, belied that faith and resorted to devote quality time for getting a mere ten-month extension. There were so many issues demanding his attention –

modernization, one rank one pay, lateral absorption of young soldiers in PSUs, war memorial construction, etc. etc. There were so many challenges to pick up, but Gen VK Singh chose something personal and was immersed deeply in it for the last six years. Over the past year, General Singh's energies have been consumed by the raging birth date controversy. There are concerns that he may have neglected his job. A December 2011 CAG report questioned the Government and the Army for not acquiring modern artillery guns for over two decades and forcing troops to rely on "obsolete 1970s vintage guns". (1.2 million strong Army handicapped by severe equipment shortages, obsolete hardware and restd in-fighting capability.)

What a waste of time, energy and resources! Army will never forgive Gen VK Singh for this callousness and self-aggrandizement. He will be remembered as a General who redefined the Chetwode saying by putting self before service.

Ironically, Gen VK Singh raised a lot of expectations by saying, "We want to set our own culture right... improve the internal health of the organisation... the Army value system has to be different from the civil society". He had also stressed that "Our core values, our ethos and tradition will receive due attention". One tended to believe his words, "An internal audit will matter a lot to me". The General identified the core values of the Army as selflessness, credentials, norms and professionalism and wanted to strengthen these. But, in contrast, he moved ahead with his single-point selfish agenda of getting his date of birth corrected. Today, Army internal health has reached its lowest ebb. Did the nation expect that his words would prove to be hollow?

Today modernisation is one of the major challenges facing the Indian Army. So, a great deal of his energies should have been spent on this high-priority area. An interesting fact is that both Gen VK Singh and his predecessor while taking over as Army Chief termed modernisation as their primary goal, but things have not moved on this front during their combined tenure.

Blatant Violation of the Army Act

Described below are some provisions of the Army Act and how they were violated by Gen VK Singh.

Army Act on False Answers on Enrolment: Any person having become subject to this Act who is discovered to have made at the time of enrolment a wilfully false answer to any question set forth in the prescribed form of enrolment which has been put to him by the enrolling officer before whom he appears for the purpose of being enrolled shall, on conviction by court-martial, be liable to suffer imprisonment for a term which may extend to five years or such less punishment as is in this Act mentioned. Gen VK Singh furnished wrong information in UPSC form.

Army Act on Undesirable Officers: An officer will not be permitted to remain in the service, if at any time during the first three years from the date of his Commission his retention is considered to be undesirable.

Had Gen VK Singh taken up the case for DOB correction soon after joining the service, the system would have understood his manipulative skills. He purposely chose not to tinker with his DOB in the first three years of his service because there was a likelihood of his falling under the category of 'undesirable officer' and he could have been removed. Being a 3rd generation officer he knew Army rules better than anybody.

Defence Services Regulation on Correspondence with High Officials: In no circumstances will officers, JCOs, WOs, OR or NCs (E) address the President, the Head of a State, a Minister, the Chief of the Army Staff, or any Army Commander, or any Principal Staff Officer at Army Headquarters, or Heads of the

Services, or any other superior formation Commander on any official or service matter except through the authorised channels.

Flouting the above rule, Col VK Singh wrote to COAS regarding my posting to Siachen. It was his face-saving attempt especially in front of his wife on whose behest all this had started. What pains me the most is that he committed to me that he would no longer pursue the case of my posting and told me to consider the case as closed. I committed the cardinal mistake of taking him on his face value. However, in the DOB row the whole country came to know that he is man of no commitment.

Army Act on Ill-treating a subordinate: Any officer, junior commissioned officer, warrant officer or non-commissioned officer who uses criminal force to or otherwise ill-treats any person subject to this Act, being his subordinate in rank or position, shall, on conviction by court martial, be liable to suffer imprisonment for a term which may extend to seven years or such less punishment as is in this Act mentioned.

My letter addressed to Col VK Singh dated 16 January 1994 vividly brings out the ill-treatment meted out to me by him. (Refer Page 61)

Army Act on False accusations: Any person subject to this Act who commits any of the following offences, that is to say:

- o Makes a false accusation against any person subject to this Act knowing or having reason to believe such accusation to be false; or
- o Refuses or by culpable neglect omits to make or send a report or return which is his duty to make or send; shall, on conviction by court martial, be liable to suffer imprisonment for a term which may extend to seven years or such less punishment as is in this Act mentioned.

Army Act on False Evidence: Any person subject to this Act who, having been duly sworn or affirmed before any court martial or other court competent under this Act to administer an oath or affirmation, makes any statement which is false, and which he either knows or believes to be false or does not believe to be true, shall, on conviction by court martial, be liable to suffer imprisonment for a term which may extend to seven years or such less punishment as is in this Act mentioned.

Gen VK Singh recommended my name for the Siachen posting, giving false evidence of myself volunteering for the same. This is the sole reason why he did not file counter affidavit when I had levelled serious allegations against him. The lapse of not filing the counter affidavit was also pointed out by the Allahabad High Court.

Defence Services Regulation on Transfers: Transfer of officers within the Regular Army will be carried out under the orders of the Chief of the Army Staff.

An application from an officer for transfer from the regiment or corps to another regiment or corps or a unit within the same corps will be forwarded to the Military Secretary through the proper channels. The application will show the officer's reason for transfer and will be accompanied by the recommendations of the CO, who will certify that the transfer recommended does not originate from any case affecting the honour, character or professional efficiency of the officer.

Initially, I was posted to Siachen Glacier on the wrong mention by Col VK Singh of myself as a volunteer for the Glacier posting. I was aghast to receive the order for my posting to 24 Rajput with change in panel. After having successfully completed my Siachen tenure with 23 Rajput, I reported back to my parent unit 2 Rajput. Within a week I was moved to 24 Rajput. It was for the first time in the history of the Indian Army that an officer was transferred in such a short span of time. The Allahabad HC judgement had come by then and it was another move of the perverted mind of Col VK Singh who once again ensured that I stay out of the battalion so that I do not unearth his misdeeds. He was afraid that I along with other officers (whom he had betrayed by fixing them in their ACR after having taken their support to fight me in the Allahabad HC) would gather more documentary proof and appeal in the Supreme Court.

Defence Services Regulation on Official Channel

(a) The authorised channel of official correspondence from a regimental officer is through the Adjutant and from the OC unit through the station, brigade/sub-area and div/area Commanders. Purely departmental matters will be sent direct to the departmental officer concerned. OCs detachments will forward all correspondence through their OCs units except on matters of purely local concern, in which case copies will be furnished to OCs units. An application from a JCO, WO and NCO will be made to his Company Commander, who, if necessary, will lay it before the CO of the unit.

Comment: The Army as an institution has clearly outlined a proper correspondence channel. But Col VK Singh cared two hoots for this channel in my case. He asked his 2IC to reply to the Army HQ explanation. The counter affidavit submitted in the Allahabad HC on my petition was not even signed by the Adjt because everyone was aware that Col VK Singh is at fault. He himself was aware of the impropriety. But why didn't the higher General officer seek his explanation? Was he so powerful at that time itself? Had every officer up the chain been vigilant about Gen VK Singh's track record, the country would not have been subjected to the DOB mess.

(b) Direct correspondence between General officers, brigade or equivalent Commanders, COs and heads of departments will be signed by such officers themselves. The general rule to be observed is that official correspondence will be conducted between equals in rank, and that any officer of junior rank corresponding with an officer of senior rank will do so through the Staff Officer of the latter.

Army Act on unbecoming conduct: Any officer, junior commissioned officer or warrant officer who behaves in a manner unbecoming his position and the character expected of him shall, on conviction by court-martial, if he is an officer, be liable to be cashiered or to suffer such less punishment as is in this Act mentioned; and, if he is a Junior Commissioned Officer or a Warrant Officer, be liable to be dismissed or to suffer such less punishment as is in this Act mentioned.

Some retired officers supported Gen VK Singh approaching the Supreme Court on the DOB issue, saying as a citizen one is within one's right to approach the court. But many people disagree saying since he was holding an office of high responsibility which is an institution in itself, he should have resigned and then approached the court for justice. By the same corollary, Gen VK Singh like any other soldier should also be tried for a court martial offence for misusing military credit note while he was CO 2 Rajput. Everyone is accountable. No one is above law.

Ideally, Gen VK Singh should have resigned and then approached the Supreme Court for seeking relief. His resignation should have been followed by a press release giving reasons of his resignation which would have exposed the DOB issue to public scrutiny and debate. This way he would have enhanced his image in the eyes of the common man. But by not resigning even on 10 Feb 2012 when the Supreme Court advised him to take back his petition he has lowered the image of the whole institution.

The reason Gen VK Singh states for not resigning is that he has unfinished tasks to attend that he had set out for himself. Hence, he says he cannot quit until he completes them. I only wish if he could let the nation know what these tasks are? Earlier, he said that if he gets time he will think about himself (regarding DOB) but within 72 hrs he moved the apex court. SC did not buy General VK Singh's argument that he will resign in 48 hours the moment Government accepts his DOB as 1951. If this was to be the case - why did he ask for all 'consequential benefits' in his petition?

Quite fast! Isn't it! Again he wants the nation to believe him that he is undertaking some tasks in organisational interest.

Misuse of MCN

A CO is responsible for proper use of all public and regimental funds. He is expected to supervise and control the committees formed for the funds management. But Col VK Singh misused*[1] two military credit notes (MCNs) for getting two generator sets from Agra Cantt station. Hav Shishu Pal Singh along with another soldier went to Agra twice to collect the generator in the second week of January 1994. I had mentioned this in my letter of 16 Jan 1994. Also it found reference in my non-stat complaint of March 10, 1994. Unique are the ways - no one enquired about the MCNs usage! I was asked to withdraw my stat complaint in which I had commented upon the misuse of MCNs, as the complete subjective report of Col VK Singh about me was expunged. An officer who was declared to be subjective in his opinion later on wrote ACRs of many many officers. How could he be considered not to be subjective with regard to other officers?

A CO is responsible for the systematic and efficient instruction of officers under his command to enable them to discharge their professional duties and also do good preparation for promotion exams. But, sadly Col VK Singh as CO was least interested in discharging this role. On the contrary, he encouraged organizing parties

1 Rightly so, he approached SC to seek justice as per rights guaranteed to him under provision of constitution. Similarly, he too should be tried for the offences (misuse of MCN) he has committed during his service like any other soldier. **Government should not shield him** by taking into consideration image of Army because at no stage he thought about image of the Army, from which he benefited the most.

every second day in the Officers Mess where one got sick of officers singing paeans to Col VK Singh and his wife. As the atmosphere in the battalion was not conducive for studies, no officer cleared the Staff College which requires intense preparation.

Tactful Use of NOO Channel: Correspondence on matters of importance, which affect more than one command and involve a principle or necessitate an alteration of regulations, are to be submitted to the Army HQ through normal channels for the decision by the Army Chief. But when I got my Siachen posting order put on hold, a reply was sought from the unit up the chain on my complaint. The complaint was against the high-headedness of Mrs VK Singh which resulted in my Siachen posting order. Col VK Singh replied tactfully under NOO and forwarded the reply under the signature of his 2IC. Who listens who cares! The Faizabad station by then had come to know about the high-headedness of his wife and how my wife was humiliated by her. Hence, he chose to put across a different dramatic perspective to higher HQ so as to influence their decision.

You have it in you!

In the past, Army Chiefs had become Field Marshals. Some were given governorship. But, Gen VK Singh possesses such qualities that can make him a political leader. We may witness another surprise from his end. He may decide to join politics because he has already given this apolitical organisation enough political colours.

Uncalled for Quandary in Army System

It was nothing but pent up grievance which he was nursing for long that made him undertake a path which made him reach to a dead-end. But in the bargain the reputation of Indian Army got bruised. The plea of his own DOB being a matter of honour cannot be easily digested. He as a Chief was to protect the reputation of his own Army which sadly he damaged by stretching his age row beyond a limit leaving little space to retreat with grace.

Gen VK Singh himself knew many years in advance that he would rise up to the post of Army Chief. That's the way succession planning is done in the armed forces. Basically, it is done to ensure the person billed to occupy the top post remains focused and thereby draw out strategies which could be given a definite shape over the years. But in the case of Gen VK Singh, if his prime focus was to get 10 months' extension, what justice he could have done to his role as a Corps Cdr or Army Cdr? Over 500 pages of statutory complaints must be the sum total of all the complaints put up by the officers in a year because generally a statutory complaint is kept brief and precise. But Gen VK Singh alone submitted nearly 550 pages stat complaints by using government machinery.

A Date to Remember

Gen VK Singh went ahead with one DOB for his promotions and another for extension of his tenure. In the wake of the DOB row, the whole succession line in the Army has momentarily stopped functioning rather thinking. This damage/effect will be there for long to be seen. Therefore, whenever any decision is to be taken, it has to be given a hard and long thought. It can't be impulsive. A correct thinking Army officer thinks over and over again before he undertakes any move or else every officer would have approached AFT for redressal of his grievance.

Can Gen VK Singh claim to be a Leader?

A leader[2] is held in high esteem and his men vouch for him, nor that his men start looking at him with suspicion. He keeps his family and personal life beyond reproach; he does not use it for furtherance of his career. Propriety is the leader's trademark. He appeals for justice and never

2 Capt **DP Kukrety's leadership** traits was par excellence. Jawans and officers stood by him when he took a principled stand against Maj VK Singh. During his jail term in Jammu he was kept in the same cell where Sheikh Abdullahji was prisoned. Everyone in the jail addressed him as 'Salam Janab'. Further more, inspite of being cashiered from service he was given military funeral by 6th Bn of Rajput regiment and was attended by Colonel of the Regiment, Lt General N.K. Kapur. He enjoyed this respect as everyone knew that due to political connections of Maj VK Singh he and his family suffered.

takes it beyond a permissible limit. The leader has no lure for the chair nor does he want to stick to it as long as he can. He stands up for the rights of his men and not for his own rights all the time.

Being someone emotionally attached with the Army as a soldier for the last few decades, I feel disappointed over the spectacle which the country witnessed over the age row. Never before people have dared comment upon the occupant of the Army Chief's office. But every Tom, Dick and Harry took unusual interest in Gen VK Singh's DOB issue thereby lowering the prestige of the Army. Here a pertinent question is why didn't he take a stand on the DOB issue when his predecessor asked him to commit on the DOB in writing? Aren't you concerned about your own office? Are you going to set this example for others to follow? Isn't the question about your office's credibility and ethics bothering your inner self?

Aren't the following views of Gen VK Singh on the age row bizarre?

- He says the 'age row' has not affected the image of the Army.
- He termed the 'age row' in Army's interest. (But the General seemed to be quite off the mark in analysing the impact of the age row as was clear from the cover headline of a leading magazine - "Self Before Service")

How do you Explain?

I was issued a warning letter dated 02 Jan 1994 to be endorsed in the ACR of period 01 Jan '93 to 31 Dec '93. The warning letter stated that I reported falsely to Bde Cdr regarding my volunteering for Siachen posting and appearing for Part D exam. Both the issues proved your malafide intention beyond doubt as was clear from the Allahabad HC judgement.

A warning letter of 28 Dec 1993 was issued in haste on a date (on 27 Dec) when I was SOS (about 13 hours advance).

Sending a copy of this letter to my next formation only confirmed the Col VK Singh's deep rooted frustration to fix me at any cost. Rightly so, the complete assessment of IO Col VK Singh was set aside owing to subjectivity.

My Prayer

In my non-stat complaint I asked for any action to be taken in the interest of the service while pointing out the following concerns:

(a) How two warning letters w/o any substantial proof were issued? Both after me being SOS (Struck Off Strength).

(b) How my Part D centre was changed?

(c) Why no explanation was sought on the misuse of government property?

(d) Why no mention of my performance in MMG competition (Div level) when a spl Part I order was published?

(e) Why no reply was given to my DO letter dt 16 Jan 1994? It contained specific allegations pertaining to misdemeanour and impropriety.

Endless questions! The supposedly fair and transparent Army system did not even bother to acknowledge this non-stat processing. If Gen VK Singh could find time from his busy visit schedule to write 500 pages of stat complaint, then am I not unjustified in asking for 50 lines of comment even today from him? If you please, sir!

Baffling and Embarrassing

The mystery of Army's no reaction to the long and continuing list of omissions by Gen VK Singh is baffling. In spite of the Allahabad HC observations against Col VK Singh, why did the Army not bother to enquire into the matter? I am of the opinion that had Col VK Singh not got emboldened by such laxity both on the part of the Army and the Ministry of Defence, he would not have brought the office of the Army Chief to disrepute. Today, courtesy the 'letter bomb' country's security position has been embarrassed. Let Official Secret Act come under play!!

The judiciary, true to its reputation, could see through Col VK Singh's dramatics in a couple of hearings in 1994. But the Army could not judge him during 40 years of his service with over 100 senior officers reporting about him. What a miss! A costly miss! Else, the Chief's office would not have been subjected to such a spectacle today!

Where is my non-stat complaint dated 10 Mar 1994? Therein, I stated clearly about the misuse of government property for the personal use of Col VK Singh. I also brought out his misleading warning letters, which later on turned out to be correct. In nutshell, I brought out his misdemeanour and impropriety and in prayer asked for:

- o To vindicate my honour set aside ACR of 1993.
- o Any other action deemed in the interest of service may also be taken.

An advance copy was sent to CAB (Complaint & Advisory Board) also. But who cares? Who listens?

Life Full Circle

Gen VK Singh's case is that he was asked to give consent by 1000 hr for the DOB confirmation. He says as Lt Gen he succumbed to pressure and he was coerced. Who will believe this!

Now take my case. I was asked by Col VK Singh at 2130 hr to obtain clearance by next day 1000 hr to proceed to Siachen on posting. Instead of reporting to "N" area for onward move, I knocked the doors of MS Branch and unhesitatingly brought out Mrs VK Singh's wrong doings, resultant of which my posting was held in abeyance[3]. My firm stance is known as 'stand for your right.' Your contention is that of an opportunist*. There is no harm in learning from subordinates. Had you taken

3 Opinion remain divided on General VK Singh filing of statutory complaint. Most of the retired officers felt that he should have resigned first and then would have approached Supreme Court. **But repeat none appreciated** that he should have continued to remain in office after SC fiasco.

a tough stance when asked to forward your consent, you would have been heralded as a brave General! Sad! You missed it!

Disposal of Grievances

- Where is my non-statutory complaint of 1994? Or since I've openly stated about the misconduct of Col VK Singh, the complaint was thrown in the dustbin?
- In stat complaint of Nov 1994, I brought out the misuse of MCN. Albeit, I withdrew the complaint as I was told that Col VK Singh's assessment had been removed being subjective. Still, why no action was taken on a court martial offence committed by Col VK Singh.
- I repeatedly brought out irregularities in mountaineering equipment purchases done but my accounts fell on deaf ears. Is there a system in place to curb corruption in the Army?

The Army proudly claims that its promotion and redressal system is fair and just 99%. I draw solace that my series of complaints fell under 1% category. How unlucky! Should I also convince myself that Gen VK Singh moving to the top in spite of all acts of impropriety forms part of this 1%? Does one have a choice not to accept it?

How Absurd?

Col VK Singh suffers immensely from superiority complex, something which Wikileaks*[4] has too revealed. During handing/taking over with 1 Maratha Li his attitude reached disgusting and demeaning proportions. When the two battalions carry out H/T over, the situation generally becomes tense if one of the COs is not mature enough.

Here are two incidents to bring out Col VK Singh's immature and childish conduct. The unit's Jonga which was modified out of regimental fund became a bone of contention between the two battalions. The CO of 1

4 The cable mentioned General Singh as an **egoist**, **self-obsessed**, **petulant** and **idiosyncratic** General, a braggadocio and a show-off, who has been disliked (and barely tolerated) by all his subordinates.

Maratha Li was not prepared to refund the exorbitant expenses incurred by 2 Rajput on Jonga modification. Following this, Col VK Singh got the Jonga top cut by iron cutter before handing over the vehicle to an NCO of 1 Maratha Li at B.D. Bari railway station. We watched in disgust and looked down since we could not face the NCO who drove the topless Jonga with a smile. Pathetic!

1 Maratha Li CO was right in his stand about not frittering away his regimental funds w/o concurrence of his officer since it was jawans' money, hence no frivolous payments could be made. Irked by the upright stand of 1 Maratha Li CO, Col VK Singh's vindictiveness reached all-time high, and he blasted a rockery (built of cement) next to the main office by 1 Maratha Li at Faizabad. He was hauled up for this unsavoury act by the Cdr.

Unheard Of!

On Col VK Singh's directions, a mess bill was forwarded to me wherein under the heading 'Personal Debt' money was deducted from my account. The deduction was on account of my using railway warrant during leave and was to be deposited in govt treasury. At no stage, any objection was ever made nor was there any ground to raise objection regarding use of railway warrant by me. Later on, the next CO directed accounts office to return the same money honourably to me, as the money was never deposited in govt treasury. As mentioned earlier, no CO of the Indian Army would stoop so low to harass his own unit officer. Has any such act of money deduction on account of railway warrant is brought out by any CO towards his own unit officer?

An anonymous complaint talks about the possible misuse of off-the-air interceptors to listen to phone conversation in the national capital. The complaint also talks about a new division created in the Army Headquarters after Gen Singh took over as Army Chief. The charter of this division's duties is not clear, but it holds widespread powers and is accused of being behind the deployment of the interceptors.

Anonymous complaints cannot be ruled out based on the premise that they are speculative and unjustified apprehensions based *inter alia* on vague and non specific allegations.

'Role: Better Half'

A gentleman officer prefers not to drive home his point by taking the name of a lady. But Col VK Singh wrote to the then Army Chief mentioning that I had developed cold feet for Siachen posting due to my wife's influence. As Anna Hazare says you view the world as you see it from your own glasses, that is, your own perspective. Similar was the case with Col VK Singh when he alluded to my wife's influence on me because he himself always remained under the influence of his wife. Officer's wives who did not get along well with Mrs VK Singh earned her wrath resultant of which many promising careers got sealed. Col VK Singh rated Maj S S Sandhu very high in his ACR in the field area. But, ironically, the very next year in a peace location Maj S S Sandhu was awarded a lukewarm ACR by Col VK Singh. It was resultant of the fact that Maj Sandhu's wife did not get along well with Mrs VK Singh. The officer remained in the same rank and took PMR gracefully – a sad end to a promising career. Here an interesting aspect is that throughout his career Col VK Singh had sought help from his wife and in-laws, hence he is deeply indebted to her and that's why she throws her weight around. On the contrary, his success mantra is – damn the world as is evident from the DOB fiasco.

Strategist Par Excellence!

Here are some key instances that prove Gen VK Singh a 'strategist par excellence' as far as his personal interests are concerned:

- Regarding my Siachen posting, Col VK Singh wrote to the then Army Chief that tomorrow anyone would volunteer and then back out. But see what did he himself do – gave commitment thrice and backed out. His excuse of being coerced into commitment was the most absurd excuse, which even a 1st termer of NDA doesn't give. All the time it was obvious that he had at the back of his mind to somehow reach South Block and then in a systematic manner get the desired change in the DOB.
- He commented on J& K situation by stating that politicians could not make headway on the gains achieved by the Army. Dr Farooq Abdullah promptly asked him to mind his business. What was the need for this comment? Just creating a hype for his own impending DOB issue?
- When the BJP wanted to hurl the Tri-Colour on 26 Jan 2011, Gen VK Singh called it a political gimmick. Does it behove an Army Chief to make such sweeping statements on political issues?
- The CRPF suffered serious casualties in Dhantewada. He blamed these casualties on their improper training, an uncalled for immature statement. Has any other PMF (Para Military Force) ever commented on the Army functioning?
- During Anna Hazare's fast at Delhi's Ramlila Maidan, Gen VK Singh gave a statement on 25 August 2011 that the country is in a morass. Within a week to add to the so-called morass, he came out with his stat complaint. Perfect timing which is key to any strategy!
- Deep in his heart, Gen VK Singh knew that he stood no chance for extension. He was just toying with the idea to achieve/bargain something which no previous chief could attain (a plump post) after retirement. Was that the real motive? Though the diversionary tactics could not fetch him 'Something Special,' the Indian Army in the process lost a lot in terms of prestige and image.
- How long will Gen VK Singh flog the Sukhna and Adarsh scams to his advantage? Is his age row anyway linked to these two scams? He in his bid to draw mileage from these issues has already washed the dirty linen in public.
- While budget session '2012 was underway, General VK Singh stated that Rs 14 crore bribe was offered. He should

give clear information without hiding the name of the lobbyist and the Company. I hope he was not playing politics by this publicity grasping tactics.

Character driven Leadership

The country has witnessed a never-before dig at the Army by the media and people courtesy the age row. Is this an aberration? Many of us think so. But we may have to rethink considering that another Army Commander, Lt Gen SR Ghosh, an aspirant to succeed Gen VK Singh, quickly got himself medically upgraded to be eligible for the post. This gentleman was earlier downgraded medically and was to earn additional pension for disability but probably the lure of another rank made him get the medical review overruled. Lt Gen SR Ghosh in his quest to become Chief forgot that such moves are seen through and in the end it is the organisation which suffers. The country needs 'morally fit' General officers who should also be medically fit. It is purely circumstantial that a subordinate of Lt Gen SR Ghosh (who was ADG then) had issued a 'To Whomsoever It May Concern' certificate to Gen VK Singh regarding his DOB.

Morally Unacceptable!

When Lt Gen VK Singh was asked to give his consent on DOB, he should have either:

- Resigned in protest.
- Sought redress by filing a statutory complaint.
- Refused to give acceptance as 1950 on DOB and faced consequences.

He carried out none of these actions which would have been in tune with the rich military traditions.

Chetwode Reminder

Umpteen times an officer goes through this saying in his military career:

The Safety, Honour and Welfare of the
Country come first, always and
every time.
The Honour, Welfare and Comfort of the
men you command come next.
Your own Ease, Comfort and Safety
come last, always and every time

Do the General officers remember the Chetwode saying? Or, immersed as they are in the five-star culture and obsessed with career advancement, they only recite the saying without intending to follow it. That's why the jawans' concerns have remained neglected for long. Jawans constitute major part of the Indian Army. They are semi-literate and come mainly from humble backgrounds. Honesty and hard work are in their blood. Sacrifice is their second name. Wearing smile on their face they brave heat, cold, storm and thunder. Fearlessly they move ahead and face bullets. They sacrifice their limbs and life willingly in the name of their paltan. One has to be part of a fighting outfit to experience all these. Every day is a challenge and new learning for one amidst jawans of a battalion. In the middle of a tough cold breezing night you find *josh* in their greeting – "Ram Ram Saheb". Admirable!

I consider myself fortunate to have been in the company of brave soldiers. Those nostalgic memories are inspiration for me in tougher times. To be very honest, my whole family fondly remembers jawans' never-say-die and selfless attitude towards life. One example of this is Sepoy Bhanwar Singh who stood by the side of Major DP Kukrety during his duel with Maj VK Singh. Displaying unflinching loyalty to Maj Kukrety, Bhanwar Singh risked his career and had forgone his pension as he was dismissed from service.

Another Army soldier, Anna Hazare, took the world by storm by displaying what does selfless service mean. Ironically, while Anna Hazare was fasting for eradication of corruption in Delhi, Gen VK Singh submitted his statutory complaint for the alleged DOB anomally purely for selfish goals. Perhaps, Gen VK Singh failed to understand that one is always remembered for the purpose behind one's role, not for the epaulettes on one's shoulders. In this regard, soldier Anna Hazare has scored over the General.

A government servant draws his pay for the month on account of services rendered by him/her as per his/her charter of duties. A Sepoy guards the border, carries out road opening party duty, etc. But here is an Army Chief who has utilized all the resources at his disposal and time to further his personal agenda to get 10 months' extension.

At times, I feel why military training cannot be made compulsory. It will benefit every individual and is bound to bring a paradigm shift in people' outlook. My friends on the civvie street must be seeing jawans' humbleness on shows on the army life on TV channels. In true sense of the word they are nation's pride. They deserve "SALUTE". Hats Off!

I have spent more than two years in the corporate world and let me confess that life of an Indian Army officer is full of challenges. Ecstatic feeling of commanding the troops, adventure activities, unseen challenges, etc. makes life fulfilling. It is an experience of the rarest kind. Each youth should go through this experience even by joining the Army for a short service commission, at least for 5 years and then leave fully equipped to take on the challenges of the corporate world for a second career and be a winner for life.

General officers are often heard saying that there is a decline in the quality of officers being recruited in the Army. When seen in the backdrop of the recent indictment of many senior officers for corruption, this statement rebounds on the General officers themselves. The rising career graph of these officers despite their questionable conduct reflects poorly on the promotion system in the Army. Otherwise, how could officers of questionable integrity rise to the General rank? A classic example is of the Army Chief Gen VK Singh who had no compunction on going back on his commitment regarding his date of birth.

Army Chief is just not another soldier. He not only occupies the highest office of the Indian Army but also personifies the institution. General VK Singh as an Army Chief overlooked this critical aspect, hence, it gives me all the more reason to write freely especially for millions of youngsters who are still mesmerized by the Chetwode saying. General VK Singh's ugly 'age row' would have an effect on the minds of lakhs of youngsters who want to join the forces. A commando, who General VK Singh is, should have dealt with Rs 14 crore bribe offer in an exemplary manner by having arrested the briber and getting him booked under 'Prevention of corruption Act'. Instead he chose like a class monitor to report it to the class teacher. How do you explain this!

To conclude, General officers must think whether they are entitled to the 'Salute,' especially in the wake of indictment of many of their colleagues for their acts of omission. The Army Chief, a retired Vice Chief and several other General officers have indulged in such acts which violated the age-old Army ethos of selfless service. Now is the right time to embark on the long overdue cleansing of the deep-rooted malaise in the Army system. If they succeed in revamping the system and making it transparent, they will restore the people's and soldiers' faith in the Army as an institution where head is held high and mind is without fear. This will undoubtedly inspire the talented Indian youth to join the armed forces. Only then the General officers will become worthy of the

General Salute

CHAPTER 8

Reforms – The Need of the Hour

"Your own ease, comfort and safety come last, always and every time." That's the last line of the Chetwode credo. But this line seems to have lost meaning or rather has been made mockery of, in the backdrop of Gen VK Singh's date of birth (DOB) row. In fact, the DOB row has caused an unprecedented damage to the Army's ethos of selfless service.

Seeing the Army Chief fighting in the Supreme Court for his baseless claims even the Jawans now feel that enough is enough. When an Army Chief while pursuing self-aggrandizement makes his prestigious office prone to ridicule by the media and common man, there could be no greater harm to the Armyman's reputation of a self-less soul. And, this has happened at a time when a good number of senior Army officers have been indicted for corruption. General officers have been found guilty of liquor scam, dry ration scam, accepting gratification for purchases and even for molesting a woman officer.

Analysts opine that lack of will to follow the Army ethos and emphasis on personal advancement stand in opposition to the necessity of making moral choices by the officers. Sincere retired and serving Army officers are worried over the upward moving corruption graph in the Army, particularly in the last few years. Retired officers say they cannot remember a time when the Army had caught so many of its Generals with their hands in the till.

Black Sheep exploiting the System Lacunae

These adverse developments prove that the Army system which vouches for fairness and transparency has failed to detect black sheep among its officers. Even the DOB row is a bizarre case because Gen VK Singh while up on his way to the post of the Army Chief must have been reported upon by at least hundred senior officers. Still he managed to steer clear of any corruption charge or controversy or remained undetected till he reached the perceived last rank of his career. And then while on the verge of retirement, the General raked up the DOB issue, just to exploit the lacunae in the system which he knew like the back of his hand. And, the system watched helplessly. Why has this happened? There could be two reasons: Either the muck is swept under the carpet or if something comes out in open, it is ensured that it remains within the confines of air-tight rooms.

What has been happening over the past few years in the Army goes against the core values – courage, competence, commitment and candour – of this patriotic institution. Straightforwardness is no more acceptable to majority of General officers. So to earn a good chit, majority of subordinate officers toe the senior officers' line and adapt to their thinking. The plea given is that to change a system you require to reach the top. But this plea doesn't hold water in the backdrop of Gen VK Singh's sole aim of self-aggrandizement during his tenure. He simply missed a golden opportunity of addressing important issues besetting the Army. Had he been straight forward in his approach, the country in general and the Army in particular would not have been subjected to the DOB fiasco. As a Lt Gen, he lacked the moral courage to pinpoint the inaccuracy in his date of birth. Now he should listen to his conscience and come out with the bribery issue in a straight forward manner and not in the manner like ... 'someone came to me, said something, it meant this, Blah..blah or else a wrong message will be sent to the outside world!

ACR–Your Purely Subjective Lifeline in Army

To keep junior officers in line, seniors have a 'terrible means' called the Annual Confidential Report (ACR) before which even the brightest and most capable officer must kneel or be scythed down. It's no exaggeration if I say that ACR is the greatest villain in the Army and its provisions have been misused by many to ruin others or take revenge. It can be likened to a snake hiding in the grass.

While annual reports are an evaluation tool in many professions, in the Army the ACR has absolute control over an officer's career. Considering that this primacy is born of the army's laudable quest for an impartial, empirical evaluation system, it is ironic that the ACR has turned into a monster of subjectivity. If the boss is unhappy with an officer – for any reason whatsoever – a single slightly adverse ACR can sink a brilliant career. This leads to rat race and compells an officer to please one's rater at any cost.

The ACR form is very elaborate and has a very large number of qualities that are required to be graded by the three senior reporting officers (the IO, the RO and the SRO). A cursory look at the ACR form will make you realise that it has everything to turn your ACR into subjective reporting.

In the Army, unlike the corporate world, there are no targets to be achieved to qualify for a good grade. Rise in one's career graph is purely based on the likes and dislikes of all the three senior reporting officers. The IO, your immediate boss, is the most important of the three reporting officers, as he feeds about you to the other two up the chain. Interestingly, sometimes your ACR depends on the likes and dislikes of "six people". The "extra three" are senior officers' "second half." (I purposely refrained from using the word "better half.")

Regarding the question of likes and dislikes, so many intangibles come into play, as listed below:

- o Are you obedient? (Misjudged for discipline)
  (To what extent!)
- o Do you look after your seniors?
  (In what manner!)
- o Is your wife participating in AWWA?
  (To the likes of the senior officer's wife!)
- o Do you follow Gandhian principles?
  (See no evil, speak no evil, hear no evil!)

So, ACR is the most important piece of paper to ascertain one's growth in Army. It can lead to a steep climb in your career or damage your growth prospects for ever. In other words, one's climb up the chain and evaluation of one's performance are prone to be highly subjective.

Guidelines on Writing ACR

The Special Army Order (SAO) giving guidelines for writing ACR is logical and lucid. As per existing instructions about ACR formulation, the IO, RO and SRO are required to include in their assessment both strong as well as weak points of the rated officer. The weak points have to be shown to the officer so that he gets an opportunity to improve his performance by overcoming his weaknesses. Or, he may represent against the said weaknesses if he feels that these remarks are not justified. The remarks of a more serious nature are termed adverse remarks while those that are not serious are called advisory remarks. The policy on advisory remarks has been long in existence and was reiterated vide Army Headquarters letter dated 21 October, 1998. The policy says:

"...Also human imperfections mean that any officer, however capable, can be advised to improve upon any trait in the quest for excellence. An officer who is clear above average bordering on outstanding can be advised to improve some facet of his personality so that he attains truly outstanding capabilities/ performance. In this context, to treat any advisory remark as 'adverse' would be a travesty of justice and completely off the mark... while adverse remarks are essential to place on record the weaknesses of the ratee, advisory remarks are also needed to bring in further improvements in the ratee's performance and overall development, though per se they may not reflect any trait of the ratee."

Based on ACRs, the promotion board draws merit list. But, how can the relative merits be assessed fairly when the assessors are different and so are the service conditions - place (peace, field, high altitude, etc), formation, task, and so on. There are far too many variables and parameters to formulate a foolproof template for ACR-based promotion. Therefore the rat race to please senior officers seems to be an unending affair. This in turn has led to a bigger mess leading to many undeserving officers making it to the General rank. Consequently, there is injustice, heartburn, humiliation and rivalry which affect the cohesiveness of a unit. Showmanship has taken precedence over professional competence. Prudence, circumspection, sincerity, honesty, probity and other positive qualities are no more virtues. In fact, the last one is an offence.

The present ACR system is based on the wrong assumption that officers up the chain of command are competent and focused towards operational efficiency of their troops. Sadly, this is far from the truth. General officers are exploiting the resources (men and material) under their command for their personal gains to please their seniors in order to obtain good chit. If a conscientious and capable junior officer objects to the same, he is sidelined and written off.

Sincere efforts should be made to ensure that writing of ACR is devoid of any extraneous consideration to make it totally unbiased. Firstly, the senior officer should be educated about how to go about endorsing the ACRs of his subordinates, and if he is still found writing subjective ACRs then he too be warned in writing about this flaw. This will serve as a warning to those officers who exploit this tool for their gains. If professional competence is given due weight in an ACR then all officers will perform without fear and contribute towards the growth of the organisation and dignified service to the country at large.

Officer-dependent ACR Grading

There are three categories of senior officers when it comes to awarding ACR grading:

- The first category is of the officers who themselves earn a 9-point report but rate their subordinates mainly as 8-point graders.
- In the second category come the officers who get an 8-point report and in turn grade their subordinates the same.
- The officers in the third category award a 9-point report (outstanding) to most deserving officers irrespective of their own grading.

To end corruption in the Army, the third-category officers are required because they always do things keeping in mind the organisational interest. They follow the Chetwode motto 'Service before Self' in true sense.

Reforms Must Right Now

Have corruption indictments and the DOB row caused an irreparable damage to the Army's noble ethos of the 'Service before Self'? Army officers generally refrain from calling corruption an epidemic. Quoting a senior Army officer, "Yes, there is corruption and we cannot live in denial." But the officer is hopeful that "the Army is too large an edifice to be irreparably hurt by corruption." Despite the officer sounding hopeful, the rising number of Army officers indicted for corruption shows that the malaise is deep-rooted. And, it does have moral and ethical implications for the Army rank and file. It is time the Army top brass took note of the moral decline of some of its officers and thought of reforms to prevent the decline turning into a cancerous disease. The reforms must aim at decentralising power and role, bringing in greater transparency and making Army officers accountable for their omissions.

Officer's Code of Honour

Ideally, the following code must govern the professional as well as personal conduct of Army officers:

- The officer's command is moral courage centric, which places every officer at the centre of ethical responsibility.
- Officer's sense of moral integrity is at the centre of his effectiveness as a leader. The advancement of one's career is never justified at the expense of violating one's sense of duty.
- All officer holds a special position of moral trust and responsibility. No officer will ever violate that trust or avoid his responsibility for any of his (advertent and inadvertent) actions regardless of the personal cost.
- Officer's foremost loyalty is to the welfare of his troops. At no cost will allow his men to be employed on a temenial task.

- o An officer will never asked his men to endure hardships or suffer dangers to which he himself is unwilling to expose.

How to go about Reforms

A serious rethinking is required to revamp the Army. It is not easy to bring change in the organisational mindset due to the following reasons:

- General officers have risen in rank courtesy the system which needs a makeover. Also, many among them do not possess the moral courage to acknowledge that the system needs reform. Some, who do acknowledge this fact, lack competence, commitment and courage required to bring in reforms, as they believe in "live and let live".
- Gutsy and outspoken officers lower down in the hierarchy cannot make changes in the system since this system moves top down. Further, if some upright and honest officers choose to stand by the good old military values, they are bound to be sidelined sooner or later.
- Sadly, today very few General officers exist who can tolerate rather understand a stand taken by a young officer in the right perspective. They behave like eccentric 'gaun bhoda' whose every word has to be honoured in letter and spirit irrespective of the consequences.

Therefore the best way to introduce reforms is:

- The media has to play an active role in shaping the public opinion towards reforms. During the height of the DOB row, a leading journal came out with a bold cover story. It was enlightening. Never heard and read before.
- The government has to institute measures to ensure that the youths in greater numbers are attracted to this noble career. An attractive salary with lucrative perks will give this profession the much needed extra edge.
- Conditions to be created for encouraging officers morally so that they could call 'spade a spade'. This will result in regular cleansing of the system and prevent clogging of communication outlets which are essential for giving

vent to one's true views on the state of affairs. This will go a long way in taking timely corrective measures.

Two Critical Aspects of Reforms

Cleansing of System: Quick disposal of impropriety cases with stern punishment is required so as to send the message that system has been cleansed. This way the best of the candidates will be attracted once again to join the elite force.

Good Officer: The good officer concept should be encouraged, not the notion of successful officer. An officer having moral courage to stand up for his troops for a right cause should be valued as he truly follows the Chetwode saying 'Service before Self.' The officers with the 'self before service' mindset should not be given importance as it has been noticed that they generally hoodwink the system. Criteria can be developed so that the Army, as per its present structure, can select its "best men for the right job". One can develop some unobtrusive indicators associated with the corporate notion of a good officer.

Importance should not be given to any officer with a perfect or near perfect record of efficiency reports. Because this officer is conforming to the existing system, which has many serious loopholes, and will have no interest in changing it. Such officers are generally seen and known to have adapted themselves well to the likes of senior officers and their wives thereby putting their subordinates at a greater disadvantage.

Performance Appraisal

Assessment system needs a serious and immediate overhaul to combat subjectivity, biases, anomalies and prejudices. Agreed, that it's difficult to put in place a system which will succeed in getting rid of ills plaguing it because the board of officers formed to review the system will be none other than those who themselves would have benefited from this system. But even small steps towards reform will serve as a deterrence against sycophancy, arbitrariness and despotic style of functioning. One day I am confident that some well-meaning retired senior officers for the benefit of the organisation will seriously consider the spirit underlying the basic principles of leadership and will come out with a fair and transparent assessment system.

The area of focus for preserving the ethos of the Army is the performance appraisal system and the selection system for promotions. The revamp of these systems is needed to engender an environmental change in the Army.

A young officer who joins the unit is all charged up and full of ideas drilled into him at the academies. But soon the realities of his vocation introduce him to an entirely different world. It doesn't take him very long to gauge the situation and understand where the focus lies, and adapt himself accordingly. In this adaptation, grooming and regimentation are prime casualties. Disillusionment sets in, the young officer, bringing with it a degree of disdain for seniors and cynicism about the values professed. However, despite some disillusioned young officers, a strong organisation like the Army can carry on for a while on the strength of its resilience. But it needs to be taken off resilience and put back on the values before things start falling apart.

The ACR-based review system can be made more objective by incorporating the following review measures:

Peer Review: The most effective review system as it provides impetus to 'regimentation' by eradicating rat-race. Most beneficial for the organisation.

Self Review: It also enhances subordinates' dignity and self respect. It tends to have a low halo error.

Upward Assessment: Will constantly keep seniors words and actions under close scrutiny. This will curb colonial behaviour.

360 Degree Feedback: It should be must for a promotion system. Amalgamation of all reviews makes for a 360 feedback. This feedback will enable the best reach the top and eliminate sycophancy and one-upmanship. Peaceful and constructive co-existence will be the norm of the day as it is nothing else but combination of all the above reviews. This should be followed as soon as possible so as to prevent undeserving officers making it to the rank of General.

Better Half for Better Things. An interesting headline about a serving Lt Gen read- 'General loses face for wife's facials'. General officers wives have always been looked upto for their charm and grace. But, few of them are also known for throwing tantrums. They throw tantrums because they are aware of the fact that the Army career rests in the hands of their husbands. They must not be allowed to meddle in the affairs handled by the officer. The Army is a sacred place for sacred duty. Its sanctity must not be vitiated by someone whose whims take precedence over the officer's operational duties.

Non Empanelment and Retirement

Everyone has to get superseded at some point or the other in his career. Accept it with grace and move on instead of clinging on to the last statutory complaint. Not worth it! It is an unfortunate development which must be arrested. If one does not get promoted, one should take it as an opportunity to change tracks. Earlier you are provided with such an opportunity better it is, as you have ample time and scope to give shape to your next career. In the present context, one remains active till about 75 years of age. This way one can make most of both the worlds (military and civil).

Here a classic example is of Lieutenant General SK Sinha, PVSM who would have become the Army Chief in 1983. But, for whatever reason, he was bypassed. He resigned and left. By doing so, he added to the dignity of the officer corps as a whole and enhanced his own personal reputation. He did not go to court despite offers by leading lawyers to fight his case.

Gen Sinha's case is just the opposite to that of a climber who generates distrust, disharmony, jealousies, stress and unhappiness in the group. Few unscrupulous officers who have known the system's weaknesses well and have total disregard for the views of their peers, seniors and subordinates go all out to extract the most from the system even at the cost of reputation of their unit. These officers in the military fraternity are termed as climbers.

OP Immediate!

Army Chief 'age row' brings to the fore another crucial issue and that is of the age factor. Army Commanders and Corps Commanders are appointed based on their age. As a result, General officers who are vying for the post of Army Chief tend to maintain a low profile so as to ensure that their candidacy doesn't get derailed. This is exactly what General VK Singh did. If his honour and integrity was in question then was he himself not responsible for his own self-esteem when he gave commitments in 2006, 2008 and 2009.

Now, when there was nothing more to gain, General VK Singh straightened his spine and stood up for his DOB. Had their been 'deep selection' process wherein the best of General is selected for the post of Corps Commander, Army Commander and Army Chief, then surely country will get bold 'decision making' Generals who will do Indian Army a lot of good. Unlike present system of age based selection which encourages Generals to take only conservative decisions involving no risk. The country needs an 'out of box' thinking General who is bold and courageous and not an opportunist.

What does Happiness Mean!

Happiness suggests that if we have the will power to control our desires and keep them limited, then our happiness quotient goes up. Lesser the denominator, that is, the number of desires entertained, higher will be our peace of mind and happiness. Happiness emanates from one's state of mind rather peace of mind. If General officers do away with 5 star culture and start living a life committed to the welfare of troops they command, then, they will make our Army a highly dignified institution.

Weightage to 'No'

It's an established fact that it is easier to say 'yes' than to say 'no'. For saying 'no,' firstly you require guts and secondly you must be prepared to face the consequences. But if General officers learn to take 'No' in their stride as they do with 'Yes', there will be no fear of consequences. But this can only be done when General officers are willing to understand strong convictions of junior officers who take principled stand for the benefit of the organisation. This will succeed in bringing out the truth leading to speedy and effective justice. If this is not promptly addressed then, as it has happened in the age row case, people from outside will start asking the Army to set its house in order.

The reform exercise would get the desired boost if truth is never hidden and the whistle-blower is not discouraged or punished. It is a pre-requisite for making this institution once again measure up to its highest ethos and traditions.

To Conclude we cannot totally isolate the Army from the open debates on various burning issues conducted by the electronic media and the growing use of RTI by people. Today the subordinates are increasingly using the redressal system to set right the wrongs done against them. Retired senior officers should urgently address the issue or an external agency may intervene. This stands to logic as the one (present serving senior officers) who wield power to do so within the Army have raised courtesy prevailing system. One major cause of discontentment among subordinate officers is the appraisal of their performance through highly subjective ACRs. It's high time that subjectivity find no place in Army decision making including writing of ACRs.

Country has witnessed in form of Army Chief age row something unprecedented – A classic case of self before service. If we have a tough system in place, then, SSG (Self Serving General) numbers will be far less in comparison to genuine and truly spirited Generals as is not the case today. The manner in which Army Chief has hogged lime light through his age row and intrigue bribe offer episode, common man is bound to question..

'is he a wrong man at the wrong place at the wrong time.'

He is heading an institution, whose reputation he had to protect. Instead, he chose to sully the image of this Army by his own irresponsible conduct. Neither does he have sense of belongingness nor any sense of responsibility.

Gen VK Singh is undoubtedly a seasoned strategist who knows how to play his cards well. After having taken a severe beating by the apex court on his 'age row' he went in for two prong strategy. Firstly, to pick up an issue of 'national security' so as to divert public attention from his age controversy and secondly bring to the fore a sensational and most sought after issue of 'corruption' by stating that he was offered Rs. 14 Crore bribe. The timing was apt to bring out both these issues as the 'budget session 2012' was on it's way. Lastly, having realised that no longer he remains a contender for 'Governor' post; there is no harm in giving political career a try.

Whatever the case may be, in the end it's the Army which has suffered irrepairable loss.

Epilogue

I would like to place on record that I am filled with a great sense of contentment after having finished writing this book. Initially I was hesitant to write this book merely because of my hectic schedule as a corporate hand. But after succeeding in balancing my official duties with book writing, now I deserve a sigh of relief!

The issues raised in this book were the ones which I wanted to vent for long. An issue left midway is far more dangerous than having not raised the issue. Leaving issues half way puts you at an uncanny ease and great discomfort and in some grievous cases pricks your conscience too. In my case, in spite of having all documentary evidence and, above all, a favourable High Court judgement, I still did not want to go to town with the story of injustice I suffered in the Army. Because I never believed in any act which could be remotely termed as vindictiveness.

Gen VK Singh relentlessly carried on with his malafide intentions in my case. I have given ample illustrations of this in the book. But when on his age issue he did not even spare the very institution from which he immensely benefitted (in fact, more than anyone in the history of the Indian Army), then I decided to lay facts bare before the people regarding the General's hypocrisy. Alongside, I also decided to bring out impropriety of few other General officers as their acts have been more than unbecoming of an officer.

There are black sheep in every organisation. Army is no exception, but still this great institution has less officers with doubtful integrity. Here it is pertinent to mention that our Army has been fortunate enough to be blessed with the services of great General officers. Fortunately, there are many General officers who follow the age-old Army ethos and values. But unfortunately, selfish conduct of Gen VK Singh led this great institution being discussed in a derogatory manner. The Code of Warrior says fight and embrace the consequences willingly but General VK Singh's role in SC, raises enough doubts over his intent to fight for honour and dignity. A Corps Commander giving the impression that he was coerced to accept the DOB, as per his daughter he was provoked - Unthinkable!. Even a Sepoy of Indian Army faces the consequences bravely rather than giving a lame excuse. An organisation which was hitherto far away from common man's criticism became an object of ridicule. People in the civvie street got a chance to cast aspersions on the spotless reputation of the Army by equating it with other professions. TV anchors got an opportunity to dig deeper and unravel certain secrets because the dirty linen was being washed in public. Some magazines came out with sarcastic cover pages on the DOB row. What a shame for an institution which even Bollywood takes care to portray in good colours! To mask his selfish interest General VK Singh has used credo of personnel honour and integrity since 'self before service' could not have been used. A timely resignation was needed to show moral protest but continuing in office on the pretext of organizational interest really begs the moral question. Also, he stated that it was his family which got affected in the age row and not the Army. But he forgot that he was head of the Indian Army and it was the Indian Army which should have been considered as his family. But, he had long ago forgotten the ethos and values of Indian Army. Unfortunate!

Gen VK Singh in an interview to a leading English journal said that his move to court on age row was needed as he had to stand up for what was correct. But did he stand up? He withdrew! A soldier fights and does not surrender. He stated that he has the right to retire gracefully. Regarding Gen VK Singh's efforts aimed at seeking extension, one fails to understand what task is left to be finished by him. Common military knowledge says that in the last couple of months of his service all Gen VK Singh will do is to traverse the length and breadth of the country in his chartered aircraft on account of his farewell visit and collect souvenirs. That's it! Agreed, but should he not answer all the questions (raised in this book and outside) regarding his personnel conduct during his Army career so as to retire gracefully. A matured conduct on his part would have saved the Army from unnecessary criticism.

An Army Chief has to be above all Prejudices

Maj General TS Handa has alleged that since he did not accede to the request of Gen VK Singh to change his DOB he had been fixed in his ACR by Gen VK Singh. In reply, Gen VK Singh says no extraneous consideration, bias and subjectivity was there while endorsing the ACR of Maj Gen TS Handa. It's difficult to believe, as in my case in the year 1994 the ACR endorsed by him was set aside owing to its subjectivity. Even before initiation of this ACR, in a complaint I had expressed apprehension about biased attitude in my ACR creeping in because of his wife's undue influence on him.

Needless to say, that every dispensation extended on the basis of parochial disposition amounts to depriving a deserving claimant his lawful rights. Merit is invariably the first casualty of parochialism as mediocre and undeserving officers get promoted. Something needs to be done to stem this rot of favoritism and nepotism in this noble profession which should be by word for discipline and true professionalism. Because of this malady which has set in many talented, professional and true leaders of merit have been sidelined and the sycophants have moved up the ladder.

It will be a sin comparing General VK Singh to legendary General KS Thimayya. General Thimayya was a man of conviction and commitment unlike General VK Singh. He had sent in his resignation to the then Prime Minister Pt Jawaharlal Nehru and was asked to withdraw. His honour was upheld and his image in front of his men grew up by several notches. On the contrary, General VK Singh is clinging on to his chair against the soldier's sentiments. He is displaying another unknown facet of leadership by blaming his own Army, his own serving and retired officers (snooping case), former Army Chief and many former colleagues. A leader is known to stand up for his men whom he commands. A leader tells his men:

'All goods are yours,
and
All bads are mine'

An Army Chief, who made it to the top post amidst controversy, fuelled controversy and is about to leave with many controversies. In my opinion, the Indian Army had never seen a Chief like this. He will be remembered for the most contentious and messiest chief's tenure. This reminds me of the saying:

*'Some people bring happiness **wherever** they go,*
*Some people bring happiness **whenever** they go'*

Troubles: Spice of Life!

In my life whenever I came to cross-roads, I chose the path laden with pitfalls despite knowing fully well that my journey on such a path would be arduous. But I loved to tackle unseen challenges posed by numerous windings and pitfalls. These challenges afforded me an opportunity to test my calibre of an army man, which made the journey interesting. Purposely, I did not take the smooth route because there was every possibility of the supposed hassle-free journey on this route turning into a nightmare. The reason being this route attracted a lot of people who wanted to avoid the tough route and created a traffic chaos.

Life is not lived in retrospection. It's mostly a journey on an uncharted course. Even if one has chalked out a roadmap to the last detail for one's own life or that of a dear one, new challenges are bound to arise no matter how hard one strives to smoothen one's life journey. Not willing to subject your life roadmap to mid-course corrections, you may turn a blind eye to these challenges. But then you will not be able to tune your roadmap to the new realities of life, thus making it irrelevant altogether. So, we all need to keep a window in our life roadmaps to accommodate challenges. After all, it is the unseen challenges or troubles that save us from becoming dormant. These add spice to our life by giving us new goals to aim for.

Words of Wisdom

The Army top brass should take a leaf out from the Supreme Court advice to judges. In 1992, the Supreme Court advised the judges: "The conduct of every judicial officer should be above reproach. He should be conscientious, studious, thorough, courteous, patient, punctual, just, impartial, fearless of public clamour, regardless of public praise, and indifferent to private, political or partisan influences."

The Supreme Court added, "He (judicial officer) should administer justice according to law, and deal with his appointment as public trust, he should not allow other affairs or his private interests to interfere with the prompt and proper performance of his judicial duties, nor should he administer office for purpose of advancing his personal ambitions or increasing his popularity."

The above words of wisdom also apply to us all in the Army. In the Army Chief's age row one expected retired General officers to come together quickly to put a lid on the whole issue rather than taking sides in TV debates and allowing the Army to face nearly a year of serious criticism and embarrassment. Today, a stage has come wherein political leaders of many parties are calling the Army Chief a disgruntled man.

Each one of us, who has donned olive green, should work towards the upliftment of this noble institution in their own little way. We all should stand up and be counted when it comes to arresting the degrading of the Army as an institution. There is an urgent need to ask harder question about the efficacy of the system. I think I have shown the way and I sincerely hope others will follow suit. This way Army top brass will take immediate note and not wait for long to address any sensitive issue. The Indian Army swears by norms. Norms are unwritten rules that get evolved due to precedents and conventions set over a period of time. Let nobody flout these norms because these are prized possession of Indian Army. Conduct of General officers in the recent past have left lot to be desired resultant of which corruption (morally and monetarily) has found roots in this great organisation. Collectively each one of us should jointly take this responsibility and since this is a recent phenomenon and is at a nascent stage. It should be nipped in the bud. This way we'll be able to win back some of our lost credibility and eroded ethos.

I am proud to be an Army man

"Jai Hind"

Index